PERFORMANCES
of SPIRAL TIME

DISSIDENT ACTS

A series edited by Macarena Gómez-Barris and Diana Taylor

A BOOK IN THE SERIES

Latin America in Translation / En Traducción / Em Tradução

Sponsored by the Duke–University of North Carolina Program in Latin American Studies

PERFORMANCES
of SPIRAL TIME

LEDA MARIA MARTINS

Translated by Bruna Barros and Jess Oliveira

Foreword by Fred Moten

Duke University Press   *Durham and London*   2025

Project Editor: Liz Smith
Designed by Courtney Leigh Richardson
Typeset in Garamond Premier Pro and Zuume
by Copperline Book Services

Library of Congress Cataloging-in-Publication Data
Names: Martins, Leda Maria, author. | Barros, Bruna, translator. |
Oliveira, Jess, translator. | Moten, Fred, writer of foreword.
Title: Performances of spiral time / Leda Maria Martins ; translated
by Bruna Barros and Jess Oliveira ; foreword by Fred Moten.
Other titles: Performances do tempo espiralar. English | Dissident acts.
Description: Durham : Duke University Press, 2025. | Series: Dissident
acts | Includes bibliographical references and index.
Identifiers: LCCN 2025008363 (print)
LCCN 2025008364 (ebook)
ISBN 9781478032557 (paperback)
ISBN 9781478029182 (hardcover)
ISBN 9781478061434 (ebook)
Subjects: LCSH: Time—Philosophy. | Space and time. | Performance
art. | Body art.
Classification: LCC BD638 .M36313 2025 (print) |
LCC BD638 (ebook) | DDC 115—dc23/eng/20250505
LC record available at https://lccn.loc.gov/2025008363
LC ebook record available at https://lccn.loc.gov/2025008364

In memoriam
MARCO RODRIGO RIBEIRO MARTINS
beloved son
still young,
embraced by Kalunga
and
ALZIRA GERMANA MARTINS
mother and queen,
sweet voice,
still irradiates

now
in the spirals
enchanted ancestors
shelter my affection
and my feelings

TO OUR ANCESTORS

Ô, com licença
Ô, com licença
Entre tambores e gungas
Ai, ai, ai
Venho pedir sua bênção

[Allow me
Allow me
With drums and gungas
Oh, oh, oh
I ask for your blessing]
— REINADO CHANT

Ajudai-me
Rainha do Mar
Ajudai-me, Rainha do Mar
Que manda na terra
Que manda no ar

[Help me
Queen of the Sea
Help me, Queen of the Sea
You who rules the earth
You who rules the air]
— REINADO CHANT

Contents

Black Swan Song

BY FRED MOTEN

If there's a body, or if here and now there must
be one, it's just a gathering of spray.
To refuse to learn, to shake his power off,
you have to find, then break, the circle of
the general twist and shout into some ribbons,
concerts of open locks brushing the ground
on every side of the ground, a cascade storm
of penetrant embrace. The spiral is
retropreformative disarmament—
a bouquet of little returns and runaways.
We can't just break the arrow of time. We have
to bury it in what we have to give,
which is what they steal because they just can't take it,
she chants. They can't survive how we survive.

Ritornellos

Performances of Spiral Time dives back into and broadens considerations on time as spirals that I have been working on since the mid-1990s. In this iteration, these concepts are interwoven with new returns, like ritornellos.[1] The compositions braid recurring ideas. They can be interpreted either sequentially, maintaining a continuous syntax, or as accumulative, complementary condensations that build upon each other. Just like call and response, they uphold the main theme while also engaging in improvisation, mirroring the nature of the inspiring spiral time itself.

Thanks to Duke University Press, especially Ken Wissoker, Macarena Gómez-Barris, and Diana Taylor, the coeditors of Dissident Acts, for having confidence in the book. I am grateful to Jess Oliveira and Bruna Barros, for their careful translation, and to Geri Augusto, for her precious comments and suggestions on the translation. I am thankful to Editora Cobogó, especially editors Isabel Diegues, José Fernando Azevedo, and Aïcha Barat, for their encouragement and affection while editing this book in Brazil.

I also acknowledge everyone who, in Brazil and abroad, has been sharing these ruminations and ideas, and those who contributed toward this publication. I, therefore, bow to those precious readings.

For me, writing is an offering. So is this book.

THEOSOPHIES, TIMES, AND THEORIES

Olê, angoma
Essa gunga vai girá
Essa gunga vai girá
Corrê mundo
Ê, corrê mar

[Ole, angoma
This gunga's gonna spin
This gunga's gonna spin
Round the world
Round the sea]
— REINADO CHANT

INSTANCES

In the body, time dances.[1] And in its movements, it initiates the being into time, inscribing it as temporality. The voice breathes from primal gestures, inspiring divine breath into beings, the original breath which circumscribes the sacred within and around itself. Before being a chronology, time is an ontology, a landscape inhabited by the body's tender ages, a wandering prior to progression, and a mode of predisposing beings in the cosmos. Time inaugurates beings in time itself, inscribing them in its kinesthetics.

FIGURE I.I. Rui Moreira, *I said* (play, part of the show *Hongolo* [Serpent's enchanter], Cia. Será Quê?, 2008). Photo: Guto Muniz.

All cultural and artistic expressions convey the worldview that constitutes and shapes societies and subjects. In embodied cultural knowledges, wisdoms of various orders manifest themselves, be they of philosophical, aesthetic, technical, or other natures, or in the most notable sociocultural events, as well as in the minimal and invisible actions of our daily lives. In everything we do, we express what we are, what pushes us, what forms us, and what makes us part of a group, a cohort, a community, a culture, and a society. Our minimal gestures and looks, the choices of our senses of taste and smell, our hearing and response to sounds, our bodily vibrations, our flourishes of language, our silences and goosebumps, our modes and ways of experimenting and questioning the cosmos, our sensibility, in all that we are and in the ways we are, we respond to cosmoperceptions that constitute us. We also respond to conceptions of time and temporalities, both in the cultural productions manifesting them and in our daily rituals.

This book explores the interrelations between body, time, performance, memory, and the production of knowledges, especially those which implement themselves through embodied practices. The idea here is that the experience and the philosophical comprehension of time can also be expressed through an inscription that is not necessarily discursive, not even narrative, though no less meaningful and efficient because of this. There is a language constituted by the body in performance, by the living body that in and of itself establishes and presents a cosmic, ontological, theoretical, and also quotidian notion of temporal apprehension and comprehension.

Ultimately, I propose as an epistemological possibility the idea that in certain cultures, time is the location of inscription of a knowledge graphed through gesture, movement, and choreography, on the surface of the skin, as well as in the rhythms and timbres of vocality. These knowledges are thus framed by a specific cosmoperception and philosophy. I explore which conception(s) of time informed and constituted the cultures and societies of the African peoples brought to the Americas, and the ways these notions were transmitted and transformed as signs of cultural formation.

If we take into account that the majority of African peoples brought to the "New World" came from societies that did not have written or printed texts as the main means of inscription and dissemination of their multiple wisdoms, we can then affirm that knowledges, from the most concrete to the most abstract, were restored and passed on through means other than those figured by writing,[2] such as oral and bodily inscriptions, that is, *graphyas* performed by the body and voice in the dynamics of movement. What is repeated in the body and voice is also an epistemic system.[3]

Ancestrality,[4] in many cultures, is a foundational concept. It is imbued in every social practice. It expresses the sense of the person and the cosmos in all their aspects, from the most intimate familiar relationships to broader and more diversified social and communal practices and expressions. In which modes, then, do this sophisticated experience of ancestrality and the immanent presence of the ancestor in the subjects' daily life inscribe a single comprehension and experience of temporality, as a *sophya*? In which ways do the times and intervals of calendars also mark and dilate the conception of a time that bends forward and backward, simultaneously, always in a process of prospection and retrospection, of simultaneous remembering and becoming?

In my understanding, spirals illustrate this perception, conception, and experience. The compositions that follow aim to contribute to the idea that time can be ontologically experienced as movements of reversibility; dilatation and contention; nonlinearity; discontinuity; contraction and relaxation; simultaneity of present, past, and future instances; as ontological and cosmological experiences that have, as the basic principle of the body, not repose as in Aristotle, but, rather, motion. In curved temporalities, time and memory are images reflecting each other.

ON THE TYRANNY OF CHRONOS

Considerations about time and the experience of temporality have always been a privileged object in philosophy, as well as in physics, anthropology, literature, and multiple areas and fields of knowledge. All cultures express diverse notions and experiences of temporalities, in their most quotidian and concrete daily lives, as well as in the most diverse theoretical, rhetorical, and ritual speculations and abstractions of their wise ones and masters.

In Western mythology—particularly in Greek mythology—there is the outline of a chronosophy interwoven into foundational texts or mythical narratives that establish chronologies. It is chronosophy in both the realm of indistinct time, non-severed from ontic chaos—time outside the conventional temporal boundaries of the creation and infancy of the cosmos, from which deities emerge—and its subsequent rupture and severance, ruled by chronologies and all their windings.

Western notions of the cosmic and theogonic formation appear, for example, in Hesiod's *Theogony*. Chronos emerges from an undetermined time-chaos that is not measurable or capturable in any sequence, order, or linearity. It is Chronos who establishes an ordered, consecutive, mensurable, and progressive generation. This introduced a calendar of deities, now organized in a determined sequential line, protected from chaos's atemporal forms and formations.

Thus, Chronos, in the West, inaugurates a certain idea of calendar-temporality by surpassing his father, instituting a linearity and a progressive lineage of substitutions and power that install and implement themselves simultaneously with the very fixation and separation of the ideas of past, present, and future. This is the opposite of his father Uranus, who is time without temporality, that is, without distinction between before and after. Chronos, in Greek mythology, is the time of severance, the time that divides itself into now and before, into today and tomorrow, instants and becomings. He opens pathways to the ascension of Zeus, his usurper-successor, his tomorrow, which is simultaneously his ontic past. Zeus, just like the future, substitutes today, the temporary and provisional present inaugurated by his father Chronos, the father of time, imposing his tyranny on the West. In his *Theogony*,[5] Hesiod graphs the Greek conception of the experience of the formation of temporality in a mythopoetic narrative that anticipates all the seductive philosophical speculation that succeeds it.

The notion of time that expresses itself through succession, substitution, and through a direction whose horizon is the future, marks Western theories about time and modernity's very idea of progress and reason, even as many philosophers from the same West problematize and argue about the lived and individual experiences of temporality. According to Reis, "The history of philosophy always had [time] as a theme: from Parmenides, Plato, Aristotle, Plotinus, St. Augustine, St. Thomas, Leibniz, Kant, Hegel, Marx, to Husserl, Heidegger, Bergson, Bachelard, to mention only the more classic discourses about time."[6]

In fact, legions of thinkers discuss time in various fields of knowledge and in fruitful and instigating elaborations. A basic paradigm and premise of these speculations lies in the assumption that time is fundamentally constituted by a chronological passage that divides and cuts it into past, present, and future. Time is then ordered in the logic of succession, that is, through instants, days, cycles, events, or happenings. The very idea of *durée*, as in Bergson,[7] would not fully escape this linear consecutive logic, even in its pulses of duration, for it does not subvert logic, but rather captures it in moments of abyssal immersion of the subject in itself. Still, according to Reis, when one "lives time, this experience already presumes a previous representation of a 'timeline'—whether circular, linear, ramified, or a combination of them all."[8]

In the images that designate time, the most graphically common one is the arrow that drives itself to the inexorability of the end and origin and, even when pointing in two directions, draws a linear mode of designation and perception of time.[9] Likewise, the image of the river that cannot be contemplated or accessed more than once, for neither the river nor the person would be the same, rushes toward the future in a continuous accelerated, non-accumulative, and irreversible flux. There, becoming is always elsewhere and the present is an illusion. The lexicon that alludes to these images is vast and includes expressions such as "before," "during," "present," "past," "future," "instant," "now," "yesterday," "today," "becoming," "duration," "repetition," "event," "succession," "simultaneity," "eternity," "conscience," "nature," which, in their web of meanings, express "temporal 'relations' or 'attributions,' that is, relations of anteriority, posteriority, and simultaneity or the succession of past, present and future events."[10] In this setup, Bosi states that each "moment that occurs is the death certificate of what is already gone," leaving only "the adjacency/imminence of the body struggling for survival."[11]

According to this lexicon, time is also configured as numeration, as a temporal sequential attribution, Chronos's domain par excellence, as Bosi summarizes well:

> For the sequential gaze, everything that succeeds brings the seal of a number disposed in a series; hence, the past moment, the previous moment, has already passed and, mathematically, cannot come back.... Thus, we begin to discuss historical time in terms of irreversibility. To this con-

ception of time belong the—only apparently contrasting—ideas of the passing of each instant and of continuation. Each minute in History lasts until it vanishes, that is, it fades away, but only to be substituted by another, and so on and so forth. This time, *when schematized*, is what was said about it, in the classic era, by Hobbes and Descartes, Newton's physics, and the philosophy that goes from Leibniz to Kant. It is *the before and after of movement* (Hobbes). It is *the number of movement* (Descartes). It is *the external measure of movement* (Newton). It is *an order of successions* (Leibniz). It is *the condition of existence of the causal order* (Kant). It is, when taken abstractly, the mensurable time of Newtonian science: t, t', t''. The time that figures in Mechanics equations, hence a number inside a series. . . . This *syntactic* view on time supports two opposite philosophies: one, that is cumulative and finalist; and the other, that is specific and, to use a neologism, contingential. In both, one may observe the model of time as seriality, succession, a chain of before-and-after.[12]

In Western thought, the very word "time" becomes an aporia.

In African philosophy, rarely quoted by Western theoreticians, multiple notions of time are also argued, and are foundational to philosophical thought. In these conceptions and fabulations, distinct from the Western, one can find arguments about time, both as theoretical speculation and as a cultural experience. Some of these notions are long-lived and classic, such as those by Mbidi, Kagame, Aguessy, Ngũgĩ, among many others.[13] Other thinkers in the African continent and in Brazil also offer us meaningful material on this vast and complex matter, for time and its experiences are also reasons for reflections in the territories mentioned above. They are also aporias. We will visit them further on. I will refer principally to the Congolese scholar and philosopher Bunseki Fu-Kiau, a great master who radiates knowledge about the history, culture, and thought of Bantu peoples, whose territorial and linguistic domains, and cosmoperception are extensive and vastly influential both on the African continent and in Brazil.

BODY-EVENT AND WORD-EVENT

In Western philosophy, it is maintained that, in the realm of language, time is expressed through words, just as it is also through words, mainly through writing, that its aporias are postulated. Time is inscribed as writing, be it in fabulation, be it in the discourse that speculates about it, as highlighted by Ricoeur, who affirms that "the *said* things are the ones inserted in their *scriptures*."[14] In his reflections on narrative and time, the philosopher will turn to Greek thought, via

FIGURE 1.2. Cyda
Moreno, *I Yellow,
Carolina Maria de
Jesus* (play, 2024).
Exhibition Women
of Words. Photo:
Ana Paula Azevedo.

Aristotle, allying the latter to Augustinian metaphysics, and gathering in both more than the teleological notions that inform and differentiate these thinkers. From Augustine, Ricoeur retrieves the very idea of the primacy of the present in Western aporia, as a vain attempt to apprehend the instant; whereas, in Aristotle, he is interested in the form of reverberation of speculation, fabulation, that is, the structure that covers the narration of time. He is interested, then, in the form of expression of the temporal experience as an argumentative, discursive reasoning.[15]

Time would be figured only by words, in its discursive expressions. In the introduction of the anthology *As culturas e o tempo*, Ricoeur states that all cultures inscribe their conception of time through words and, in this particular anthology, all the authors "insist on the adherence of the conception of time and history to the settings of language."[16] From this perspective, the empirical perception of time, according to Ricoeur, would be inseparable from its discursive translation, even if it is presented in a hymn, "in its hymnic mode."[17] He reiterates:

> The *diversity* of cultures comes from the diversities of languages in a broader, but maybe deeper sense than the simple diversity of words and syntaxes, and even than the—more literary—diversity of the forms of discourse (hymn, chronicle, epic, tragedy, and lyricism). Many of the cultures considered in this anthology have their implicit or explicit conceptions of time linked to the emergence of a Word—or Scripture—which creates, in benefit of an event of foundational discourse, the set of experiences, behaviors, and interpretations that, in turn, constitute the unique characteristic experience of that culture.[18]

According to this line of reasoning, writing, as a place of memory, is one of the most praised means of expression and underwrites the West's favored places of memory, for, according to Merleau-Ponty, "what we call 'ideas' are carried into the world of existence by their instruments of expression—books, museums, musical scores, scriptures."[19] These are the platforms and devices favored by the West for keeping memory. Even though Ricoeur links rites explicitly to what he calls "word event," by stating that "so the diversity of exegetic intelligence is the imperious corollary of the word event," he will recognize the power of rites in the perception of time, for, according to him, "time is not only interpreted, but signified by the rite."[20]

This way of thinking about time as a narrative instance, subject to a function of narration, underwrites many formulations of countless other thinkers, who highlight them in varied genres and forms from the most diverse cultures and societies, through which time—and its heuristic and holistic notion; empirical understanding; ontological experience; cosmic, functional, everyday representation; and figuration in clocks and calendars—is narrated through the written word.[21]

However, within Western societies, other ways of conceiving, experiencing, and living time, as well as expressing it as language, survive. Within the very realm of the aesthetic experience of the word, time provides rhythm to one of the most beautiful forms of human expression and transgression of its conception as an absolute linearity: the poetic language, whether that of poetry or that of myths.

Poetry is time. Time as a ritornello, dispersed in a rhythmic spatiality. As Bosi teaches us, the poetic discourse presupposes recurrences, resonances, turns, cycle regimes, return procedures, the simultaneity of several times and their reversibility. "Poetic discourse," Bosi would say, "as a fabric made of sounds, lives a regime of cycles," a coming and going processed as rhythm, phonetic subsystem, intonation, timbre, duration, tempos. With these modes of ritornellos, poetic time disrupts and breaks the absolute sequential line, interweaving curves and spirals and thus, through the "cycle that closes and through the waves that come and go, the poem summarizes and rounds off discourse's successive temporal line."[22] He adds: "Rhyme and rhythm are procedures of returning, of bending, of internal reversibility. They are structure."[23]

Still, according to Bosi, the "mythical time and the time of worship of the dead are also characterized by being a (*com*)position of recurrences and analogies. Their main note is reversibility. A structural reversibility, for it embraces internal returns."[24] This also breaks the logic of the productive economy, in which one cannot waste time, because if "economy works according to a game that aligns the mechanisms of production, supply, and demand, arranging them in series, and therefore measuring them (since time 'is worth' production which, in turn, is worth money), this does not mean that this logic is the only interactive rule steadily bringing men together in society."[25]

In the same anthology where Ricoeur reaffirms that in all societies, temporal experience is expressed through the written word, he also presents, albeit with some bewilderment, several theorists who discuss some absolutely unique conceptions of temporality in relation to Western perspectives. This list includes the Hindu, the Chinese, and the African conceptions, all of which process very diverse and contradictory notions to the ideas of time expressed through succession, through substitution, through a defined origin of progressive direction and meanings whose horizon is an often apocalyptic inexorable end, as in the Judeo-Christian tradition.

In countless contemplations regarding time, the word holds a unique place. Not everything, however, seems to be conveyed and expressed solely by words, in its status as writings. African notions of time, for instance, emphasize the uttered word as a *locus* of expression of temporal experiences. This concept is situated within a wide spectrum of phonic and sound elaboration within languages, processed by the body, aligned and composed by other perceptions that translate them in and through the body.

African philosophy takes into account the entire range of knowledges regarding oral performance as significant for the inscription of temporality experiences, as well as for their epistemic elaboration. The word as *oralitura* inscribes itself on the body and in all its activities.[26] And it produces knowledge, in spite of the declared biases of European thought, which disqualified Africa as a thinking continent. This type of exclusionary reasoning is largely due to the false dichotomy between orality and writing emphasized by the West. This biased view favors written discursive language as an exclusive and privileged mode of postulating and expanding knowledge. This mode is implemented due to the primacy of a linear progressive conception of time and is established as thought due to the almost absolute dominance of alphabetic writing as a platform of fixed *graphyas* in its narratology and its writing, ignoring or neglecting other modes of establishing wisdoms, including those made up by voice and its resonances in various embodiments. As Finnegan also states: "So it is that when we are faced with any art in which words play a part at all, we so readily look to its textual *writable* qualities. . . . It is language furthermore, above all in its written form, which is so often conceptualized as the vehicle for modernity, rationality and the value of the intellect. In this still strikingly prevalent ideology, written language (especially when alphabetically printed) stands for the highest achievement of humanity."[27] According to the logic of Western reason, writing would translate one of the modes of recognition of the historical subject and of historicity, as observed by Pomian:

> Throughout the 19th century, both philosophers of history and professional historians conceived time as merely linear. . . . Linear, cumulative, and irreversible time is equated with the time of history to such an extent that the peoples in which it cannot be found are simply peoples without history, *Naturvölker*. On an ideological level, the equation of historical time with linear time . . . is a component of Eurocentrism. . . . Sometimes, even within Europe, it justifies the division between peoples who have a history and those who are deprived of it; it justifies the feeling of superiority we get when we turn to the past and compare it to the present.[28]

This hegemonic thought, a devaluation of the African continent, is present in Hegel's ideas about it: "Africa is no historical part of the world, it has no movement or development to exhibit . . . the unhistorical, undeveloped spirit, still involved in the conditions of mere nature . . . as on the threshold of the world's history."[29]

In the colonial system, the emphasis on writing prolongs this illusory dichotomy between what is oral and what is written, with the latter actually becoming an instrument of domination practices, unequal power relations, and strategies for excluding the peoples who favored bodily performances as forms of creation, memorization, and expansion of knowledge.

Africa has always had written and oral textuality, but without a hierarchy of modes of inscription, even in the oldest writing systems, such as the Egyptian system, which, along with Sumerian and Chinese systems, is one of the oldest, besides other centuries-old writing systems such as "the Bamoun (Cameroon) . . . Vai (Sierra Leone), Nsibidi (Calabar, western [*sic*] Nigeria), Basa and

Mende scripts (Sierra Leone and Liberia),"[30] besides those originating, in the Middle Ages, from Islam, informs Aguessy. According to this author, "every human society, as is now widely recognized, has some specific means of recording that permits it to appropriate time, to a certain extent" and, in Africa, "cultural values have by and large been transmitted and perpetuated orally." Aguessy concludes: "Therefore when I speak of 'orality' as being characteristic of the field of African culture, I mean that it is preponderant, not exclusive. I use the term to indicate that the oral transmission of knowledge and cultural values is generally preferred, but this need not exclude a specific mode of recording and stabilizing messages."[31] The prevalence of literacy, and the consequent high status of writing, introduced both in Africa and in the Americas by European colonizers, did not just substitute one mode of inscription with another. The mastery of writing was instrumental in the attempt to erase wisdoms deemed heretical and undesirable by Europeans. When literate writing was turned into an exclusive source of knowledge, its domain superimposed itself, neglected, and tried to abolish other systems and contents that were not considered by the colonizer as qualitative knowledge, or even as knowledge. The domain of few, as it excluded, marginalized, and alienated what was once familiar. It disturbed the colonized societies, shifting power relations among subjugated peoples. Alphabetic writing installed itself as an instrumental vehicle of ostracism: It segregated and stigmatized. It was not an addition or a supplement, but rather an imposition, an exclusive means of diffusion, as were the values it disseminated, whether social, religious, behavioral, or related to worldviews. The civilization of writing, of books, imposed itself, as if it were unique, true, and universal in its yearning for domination and hegemony, and it was resistant to any difference. It also aimed at the symbolic or literal disappearance of the other, at its erasure. Taylor points out that "what changed with the Conquest was not that writing displaced embodied practice (we need only remember that the friars brought their own embodied practices) but the degree of legitimization of writing over other epistemic and mnemonic systems."[32]

Despite this repression, what history shows us is that even though the performative practices of Indigenous and African peoples were prohibited, demonized, coerced, and excluded, these same practices ensured, through various processes of restoration and resistance, the survival of a *corpora* of knowledge that resisted attempts at annihilation, whether through disguising, through transformation, or through the innumerable modes of revitalization that nuanced the whole formation process of the hybrid American cultures.

These embodied practices, alongside the exercise of writing—a privilege of few—shaped the new cultures and societies in the Americas through a process of mutual influences, just as European knowledge entered the universes of African and Indigenous peoples. It became a two-way path: European knowledge was also affected by Indigenous and African peoples, even though, in the hierarchy of power, the latter did not, and still do not, enjoy the same degree of legitimacy, recognition, or primacy. According to Roach, "echoes in the bone refer not only to a history of forgetting, but to a strategy of empowering the living through the performance of memory,"[33] because, despite the centralizing European self-consciousness, Africa "leaves its historic traces amid the incomplete erasures, beneath the superscriptions, and within the layered palimpsests."[34]

The African cultures transferred to the Americas found in orality their favored —albeit not exclusive—way of producing knowledge. Likewise, for the peoples of the forests, the production, inscription, and dissemination of knowledge took place primarily through bodily performances, rites, songs, dances, and synesthetic and kinesthetic ceremonies. Through these performances, a plethora of knowledge was transmitted by the body in movement and its vocality, from simpler behaviors, practices, and daily habits, to the more sophisticated techniques, forms, cognitive processes, and more abstract and sophisticated thinking, including their cosmoperception or philosophy.

Graphing wisdom was not, then, synonymous with mastery of a language alphabetically written. Rather, graphing wisdom was indeed synonymous with an embodied experience, with an embodied knowledge that found its place and environment for inscription in the body in performance. Words were danced, gestures sung, every movement resonated with a choreography of the voice, a pronounced score, a pigmentation graphed on the skin, a sonority of colors.

The body becomes an auratic wisdom, a rhythmic calligraphy, a *corpora* of knowledge. In one of the oldest records of Toltec wisdom, the installation of a new city did not begin when the dwellings, streets, and temples were finished, but rather and only when the chants and music were heard, and when the drums were beat. Singing and dancing. This is how that place and civilization were founded. As León-Portilla states, "It is beautifully stated in the Indigenous text that all these cities [Teotihuacan, Azcapotzalco, Culhuacan, Chalco, Xochimilco, among many others] came into existence only when music was established in them."[35] And so they poetically told us, while singing:

Se estableció el canto
se fijaran los tambores, se dijo que así
principiaban las ciudades:
existía en ellas la música.[36]

[And then there was singing,
the drums were played, it was said it was like this
that cities began;
there was music in them.]

One of the chants by the *congadeiros* (Congado practitioners), in Minas Gerais, reminds us of this same multi-significant preeminent relationship between Black peoples and chants:

Cheguei na casa do rei
O meu destino é cantar
Sá rainha me falou
Pisa neste chão devagar

[I arrived at the king's house
To sing is my destiny
The queen told me
To step on this ground carefully]
— REINADO CHANT

CROSSED *NZILAS*, PERFORMANCE, AND *ORALITURAS*

Inscriptions of knowledge via embodiment are sought in various areas through alternate and alternative epistemologies and perspectives.[37] Many scholars ponder over other possible means of approaching embodied wisdoms, proposing different theoretical approaches to their intellectual actualization and apprehension. Performance Studies, for example, as a multidisciplinary field, breaks the sterile dichotomy between oralities and writing, providing us with methodological tools for the investigation of performance practices.

Performances, for Schechner, are "marked, framed, or heightened behavior separated out from just 'living life'—restored restored behavior." As such, the so-called *twice-behaved behavior* can be "actions marked off by aesthetic convention as in theater, dance, and music,"[38] in habits and social conventions, and in the most diverse cultural practices, whether in the realm of the sacred or in the realm of the profane in rites, ceremonies, and other practices, no matter if considered aesthetic or not. Still, according to Schechner, the restored behavior "can be worked on, stored and recalled, played with, made into something else, transmitted, and transformed,"[39] always through a symbolic and reflexive frame, whose "meanings need to be decoded by those in the know,"[40] that is, twice-behaved behavior, which alludes to the reiteration of the performed action, its repetition in time and as time and duration, as well as its simultaneous ephemerality.

This definition of performance, always *in progress*, that is found in numerous texts by this author, alludes to some basic assumptions for its understanding, namely: "A performance [even when it emerges from a painting or a novel] takes place as action, interaction, and relation."[41] "The habits, rituals, and routines of life are restored behaviors" and, as such, are alive and can be recreated and rearranged. They "can be of long duration as in ritual performances, or of short duration as in fleeting gestures such as waving goodbye."[42] Their symbolic and reflective universe of meaning demands the mastery of the codes, including cultural ones, that inform them.

The concept of performance as "restored behavior" implies the idea of a permanent but ephemeral repetition that never makes itself known nor repeats itself in the same way. According to Roach, ephemeral and durable performances are not "prior to language, but constitutive of it."[43] We can point out, along with these intellectuals, that performances themselves, as well as Performance Studies, allow us to shift the *focus* from written text to the broad and significant repertoire of embodied wisdoms.[44]

For Taylor, performance "on one level, constitutes the object/process of analysis in Performance Studies, that is, the many practices and events—dance, theater, ritual, political rallies, funerals—that involve theatrical, rehearsed, or conventional/event appropriate behaviors."[45] As such, the term *performance* is inclusive and covers a wide range of actions and events that require the living presence of the subject for their realization and/or enjoyment, functioning as acts of transfer, since, on a certain level, "performances function as vital acts of transfer, transmitting social knowledge, memory, and a sense of identity through reiterated [behavior]."[46] On another level of apprehension, "performance also constitutes the methodological lens,"[47] which enables us to analyze certain events as performance, since, theoretically, "as a term [performance] simultaneously [connotes] a process, a praxis, an episteme, a mode of transmission, an accomplishment, and a means of intervening in the world." That is, performances are and build epistemologies.[48]

Within the scope of French theories, Paul Zumthor also offers a series of insights that aid us in thinking about the performances of orality. He does so by providing substantial inflections for their understanding, analysis, and reception. His contributions to the poetics of the voice, the body, performative gestures, and the reception of oral transmission performances highlight, among other aspects, the notion of performance as a "knowing how to be," a "knowledge that implies and commands a presence and a conduct, a *Dasein* comprising concrete space-time and physio-psychic coordinates, an order of values embodied in a living body."[49]

Connerton uses a series of examples through which we can glimpse many sociocultural activities that typify social memory, from the most naive—and apparently bucolic and playful—to those that carry philosophical concepts and wisdoms within them through conventional practices, repeated in collective events of greater or lesser size, in the public and official or in private spaces, in urban and rural communities, in festive, celebratory, or incantation rites, and even in the costumes that compose the body. According to him, "concerning social memory, we may note that images of the past commonly legitimate a present social order."[50] Thus, we may say that our experiences of the present largely depend on our knowledge of the past.[51] He adds that "social habits are essentially legitimating performances. And if habit-memory is inherently performative, then habit-memory must be distinctively social-performative."[52] Commemorative ceremonies, for instance, "prove to be commemorative only insofar as they are performative; this is performed knowledge."[53]

From this perspective, as Pierre Nora also warns us,[54] the memory of knowledge is not only safeguarded in sites of memory (*lieux de mémoire*), libraries, museums, archives, official monuments, theme parks, et cetera, but is constantly recreated and transmitted by environments of memory (*milieux de mémoire*). These are oral and bodily repertoires, gestures, and habits whose transmission techniques and procedures are means for creating, passing on, reproducing, and preserving knowledge.

In Brazil, many intellectuals are seminal for the analysis and understanding of our embodied knowledge. Several of them will be mentioned and consulted throughout the following pages. In my case, I have worked with the term *oralitura* since 1997 in order to allude to some modes and means by which—in the realm of performative practices—gesture and voice modulate the *graphya* of embodied knowledges. These include various orders and diverse natures, including philosophical knowledge, in particular, an alternate and alternative conception of time, its reverberations, its impressions and *graphyas* in our ways of being, proceeding, acting, fabulating, thinking, and desiring.

Conceptually and methodologically, *oralitura* designates the complex texture of oral and bodily performances, their functioning, processes, procedures, means, and systems of inscription of the knowledge founded by and foundational to bodily epistemes. The term highlights the transit of memory, history, worldviews, and multiple epistemes that are processed through embodiments in such performances. It also alludes to the *graphya* of these wisdoms, as performative inscriptions and as a crossing out of the dichotomy between orality and writing. *Oralitura* belongs to the realm of performance and its agency. It allows us to approach, theoretically and methodologically, performance's protocols, codes, and systems, the modus operandi of its realization, reception, and affectations, as well as its techniques and cultural conventions, such as the inscription and *graphya* of wisdoms.

In the realm of *oralitura*, not only rituals gravitate, but also a great variety of formulations and conventions that install, fix, revise, and disseminate themselves through countless means of performative cognition, while also graphing—through a body infused with sounds, vocalities, gestures, choreographies, accessories, drawings and graffiti, traces and colors, knowledges and flavors, values of multiple orders and magnitudes—African-inspired logos and gnoses, as well as multiple possibilities for the crossing out of exclusionary and discretionary protocols and fixation systems.[55]

All these authors, with greater or lesser emphasis, allude to the fact that all societies and all cultures have their ways and means of remembering their knowledges and their practices, by developing processes for maintaining their cognitive collections and even questioning, revising, and reshaping them. Certainly, these practices underwrite the most intimate place in social relations and in the subjectivities of the individuals who form and practice them, in all spaces and contexts of interrelationships around which knowledges and values of multiple natures and magnitudes gravitate, including a conception of time and temporalities: the spiral time.

In the context of the thought that entwines diverse and different African cultures with the cultures of the diaspora, movements of retroaction and simultaneous advances can only be measured and argued within a worldview and a conception of the experience of time and temporalities initiated by a guiding thought; that is: ancestrality, the mater principle interrelating everything that exists in the cosmos, transmitting the vital energy that guarantees the concomitantly similar and different existences of all beings and everything in the cosmos. It is the extension of curvilinear temporalities, governing the implementation of cultural practices, underwitten by a non-severed time that cannot be measured by the Western model of linear and progressive evolution. A time that does not elide chronology, but subverts it. A curved, reversible, transversal, long-lived, and simultaneously inaugural time, a *sophya* and a chronosophy in spirals.

THE CURVED TIMES
OF MEMORY

Diâdi nza-Kôngo kandongila: Mono i kadi kia dingo-dingo (kwènda-vutukisa) kinzungi-dila ye didi dia ngolo zanzîngila. Ngiena, kadi yateka kala ye kalulula ye ngina vutuka kala ye kalulula.

[Here is what the Kongolese Cosmology taught me: I am going-and-coming-back-being around the center of vital forces. I am because I was and re-was before, and that I will be and re-be again.] — BUNSEKI FU-KIAU, *African Cosmology of the Bântu-Kôngo*

AFRICAS

In all its diversity, Africa imprints arabesques and styles on American cultures, inscribing itself in palimpsests that transcreate and perform its presence in the Americas through numerous processes of cognition, assertion, and formal and conceptual metamorphosis. Arts and cultural constructs infused by African and Indigenous wisdoms reveal the ingenious and arduous means of survival of this heritage during the centuries of systematic social and cultural repression of the African memory, which was transported to American territories via the circum-Atlantic diaspora and other transcultural and transnational routes and relations.

Through multiple and rhizomatic palimpsests, Africa impregnates the Americas. For, as Domingos Mourão—the Old Portuguese, one of Mia Couto's *Under the Frangipani*'s narrators—states, "Africa robs us of our identity. But at the

FIGURE 2.1. Sanara Rocha, *Performance: By Memory and Fire, Iyá Ilu*, 2017.

same time as it empties us, it fills our being."[1] In the Americas, many of the basic principles of Black gnosis, its epistemic systems, and a complex collection of knowledges and values were reterritorialized, reimplanted, reinitiated, recycled, reinvented, and reinterpreted in the countless historical crossroads derived from these crossings.

Black culture in the Americas is double-faced, double-voiced; it expresses—in its foundational constitutive modes—the disjunction between what the social system presumed that subjects should say and do and what, through countless practices, they have actually said and done. Displacement, metamorphosis, and re/covering are some of the basic principles and tactics operating in the cultural formation of the Americas, in this operation of asymmetrical balance.

And there are many readjustment processes. Some examples are the replacement of typical African raw materials with similar local materials, the manufacturing of musical instruments with recycled materials, and the production of natural plant-based pigments to dye fabrics and ornaments that were also made with native materials and plants. In the United States, for example, "where the use of the African drum was strictly forbidden," its reinvention was exemplary. There, "other percussive devices had to be found, like the empty oil drums that led to the development of the West Indian steel bands. Or the metal wash basin turned upside down and floated in another basin that sounds, when beaten, like an African hollow-log drum. The Negro's way in this part of the Western world was adaptation and reinterpretation. The *banjo* (an African word) is an African instrument, and the xylophone, used now in all Western concert orchestras, was also brought over by the Africans."[2] This also happened in other regions of the Americas, such as Brazil and the Caribbean, where enslaved Black people, defying prohibitions and, to some extent, overcoming inhospitality in an alien and adverse landscape, made their sacred drums out of trunks, leaves, and vines, and used Job's tears and other materials found in the American geographies instead of *Opeles* and other accessories.[3] With instrumental and sophisticated techniques, these modes of adaptation, substitution, production, and invention recover stylistic-cultural traits, reframe the environment, and bestow power to the person.

Opposing the supposed primacy of writing and verbal discourse, Roach claims that "texts may obscure what performance tends to reveal."[4] Thus, ritual performances, ceremonies, and celebrations, for example, are fruitful memory environments of the vast repertoires of mnemonic reserves, kinesthetic actions, patterns, and cultural techniques and procedures recreated, restored, and expressed in and by the body. In this perspective, the ritual performative act does more than evoke the semantic and symbolic realm of the double repetition of a re-presented action; it constitutes, in itself, action itself.

Ritual ceremonies occupy a unique and privileged place in the formation of Black cultures: as sites and environments of memory, they recreate and transmit gestures and habits, as well as forms and techniques of creation and transmission, through oral and bodily repertoires. They are records and means of identity construction, transcreation, and knowledge protection. Rites transmit and implement aesthetic, philosophical, metaphysical—and other—wisdoms, either through their symbolic framework, or through the modes of utterance, devices, and conventions that sculpt their performances. Júlio Tavares says:

> Even if one recognizes the impossibility of speaking of a universal, essential, static, and structural pattern in all the extension and repetition of these forms of life, it is certainly believed that we can speak of a "family of similarities." This means reiterating the existence of occasional regularities, in which the "rite" is what draws closer as the constant element, the communicational and repetitive element in the dynamics of the process, the distinctive element in the everyday activity of movement-making, the gesture, the voice, the rhythm, and the elaboration of a body language in its

ways of producing presence and movement. It is in the intersection and articulation of these elements in the making of the ritual act that the unity of language, aesthetics, ethics, thought, and meaning operates. The body appears as a powerful manifesto of multiple scenarios and as the background-figure of the whole process in which it consistently acts to evoke the state of being, the condition of being, and the manifestation of thought.[5]

The memory of knowledge is implemented in and through ritual performance, through performance techniques and procedures conveyed by the body. In the ritual realm, in multiple forms—chants/songs, dances, costumes, accessories, ceremonial objects, scenarios, processions, and celebrations—and under a philosophical and religious cosmoperception, performances reorganize textual, historical, sensory, organic, and conceptual repertoires of distant Africa. They reorganize the scores of African knowledge and wisdom, the alternate body of recreated identities, memories, and reminiscences—that is, the corpus of memory that carves out and crosses diaspora-generated voids and gaps. Rites fulfill an exemplary paradigmatic pedagogical function, as a model and index of change and displacement; for, according to Turner, "as a *'model for,'* a ritual can anticipate, even generate change; as a *'model of,'* it may inscribe order in the minds, hearts, and wills of those who take part in it."[6]

Many African intellectuals highlight the constituent interaction of people with the environment; the bonds between physical, material, and spiritual dimensions; the idea that there is life and a meaningful existence in minerals, in fauna and flora, in gasses, and in the many states of water, in all beings, including humans. This complex network of perceptions about the cosmos, this collection of wisdoms, fundamental components of African cosmoperceptions, crossed the ocean sea. According to Honorat Aguessy, "A *proprium africanum* . . . must take into account the different cultural inflections produced by the following three types of variables: the physical, the socio-economic and the historical."[7] The historical movement of these wisdoms is quintessential when we reflect on the African *continuum* of African traditions in the Americas. Here, the meanings of intercultural and transcultural transit, and the meanings of *kinesis*, transformations, and permanences are keys to its apprehension. Aguessy states:

Tradition, contrary to one's static idea of it, is in no way the mere repetition of identical sequences; by no means does it reflect a petrified state of culture which is transmitted without change from one generation to the next. Activity and change are inherent in the concept of tradition. . . . African societies evolve within a framework; the migration of its groups constituting both a significant metaphor and a significant metonymy of this fact. Even in the midst of population movements or changes, which are synonymous with dialectical enrichment, the individual never ceases to be welded to the community.[8]

Tradition, according to Aguessy, "is not a passing thing," nor "a force of inertia." On the contrary. Tradition and the *proprium africanum* "reveal [themselves] in the most contemporary behavior as well as in the most ancient gestures, in the simplest and most deliberate physical occupations as well as in purely intellectual undertakings, in relations between people as well as in individual attitudes."[9] Our wise Mestre Didi also teaches us: "When I speak of Tradition, I am not referring to something frozen, static, indicating merely anteriority or antiquity, but rather to the mythical inaugural principles which constitute and guide identity and memory, capable of transmitting essential continuity from generation to generation and, at the same time, re-elaborating themselves in different historical circumstances, incorporating aesthetic information that allows for the renewal of experience, strengthening their own values."[10]

THE RISKS OF THE CROSSROADS

Black peoples are constituted at the crossroads of these multiple and polysemic wisdoms. The Brazilian cultural fabric is informed by processes of transnational, multiethnic, and multilingual crossings that generate multiple vernacular formations—some wearing new faces and others mimicking, with some subtle differences, old styles. Trying to better apprehend the dynamic variety of these processes of transit, interactions, and intersections, since 1991 I have been using the notion of "crossroads" as a concept and semiotic operation that allows us to carve out the forms that emerge from such processes.[11]

In the philosophical conception of many African and African Brazilian cultures and their respective religions, the crossroads is the sacred place of mediation between multiple systems and instances of knowledge, often translated into a cosmogram that points to the circular movement of the cosmos and of the human spirit that gravitate around the circumference of its intersections. It is, then, as thought and action, a locus of challenges and twists; compression and dispersion; an iconic spatiality that illustrates the countless and diverse movements of revitalization, improvisation, and settling of cultural and social expressions, including aesthetic and political ones, in their broad sense and spectrums.

A foundation of thought and action, the crossroads acts as a translator and operator of the principles that structure Black thought. It is the founding cartography for the epistemology circumscribed by African and African diasporic wisdoms. It also offers us the possibility of interpreting the systemic and epistemic transit that emerges from intercultural and transcultural processes, in which performative practices, conceptions, and worldviews, as well as philosophical and metaphysical principles and multiple wisdoms—sometimes disagreeably—confront and intersect each other.

In the ritual realm—therefore, in the performance realm—the crossroads is a radial place of centering and decentering, intersection and deviation, text and translation, confluence and amendment, influence and divergence, fusion and rupture, multiplicity and convergence, unity and plurality, origin and circulation. An operator of performative and discursive languages, the crossroads, as a third place, is the generator of diversified signifying production and, therefore, of plural meanings. In this conception of crossroads, one can also find the kinesthetic and changeable nature of this enunciative and performative instance of implemented wisdoms.[12]

Black culture is a crossroads culture. In African discursive and philosophical elaborations as well as in its cultural expressions, the notion of crossroads is a nodal point that finds a complex formulation in the Yoruba philosophical-religious system. Èṣù Elegbara, the lord of crossroads, doors, and borders, the dynamic mediator principle of all acts of creation and interpretation of knowledge, reigns in the intersections. As a mediator, Èṣù is the communication channel that interprets the will of the gods, that brings human desires to them. In mythological narratives, more than a simple character, Èṣù appears as a messenger who inaugurates narration itself. Juana Elbein dos Santos highlights the communicative and mobilizing functions of Èṣù Bara, dynamic principles of the Nago philosophical wisdom in Brazil:

> Èṣù is not only related to female and male ancestors and their collective representations, he is also a constitutive element, the dynamic element, not only of all supernatural beings, but also of everything that exists. In this sense, like Ọlọrun, the supreme entity, the universe's protomatter, Èṣù cannot be isolated or classified in any category. It is a principle and, like the àṣẹ he represents and conveys, he necessarily participates in everything. Since Èṣù is the dynamic and expansive principle of everything that exists, without him all the elements of the system and its becoming would be rendered static, life would not develop. . . . Just as Ọlọrun represents the principle of generic existence, Èṣù is the principle of differentiated existence due to his role as a dynamic element that leads him to propel, develop, mobilize, grow, transform, and communicate.[13]

As an agent of the entire process of semiosis, and, therefore, of the production and communication of meaning, Èṣù Òjíṣè is also known as the "interpreter and linguist of the system,"[14] the one who keeps the àṣẹ—the logos, according to Henry Louis Gates Jr.[15]—with which Olódùmarè created the universe. His various names translate his spiral multiplicity and his nature as a driving principle. Gates also points out that, in the syntax of the Yoruba sign interpretation system, governed by the deity Ifá, Èṣù functions as the principle from which emerges the possibilities of creation and translation of knowledge. In the rhetorical structure of Ifá's interpretive process, Èṣù "[connects] truth and understanding, the sacred and the profane, the text with interpretation, the word (as a form of the verb *to be*) that links a subject with its predicate. He connects the grammar of divination with its rhetorical structures."[16]

Èṣù is what presents and settles the ontology of time in Yoruba cosmogony, because he is ontology itself, the time that simultaneously curves forward and backward, which is, as Sodré teaches us, its own "setting and rising."

> This means that the event manifests itself by inaugurating something new in the present, but it does so in a dynamic of retrospection (the past that changes) and prospection, which takes place in the "[act of] making [something] possible." In other words, this event is not temporal in itself; that is, it is not found on a defined horizon, but it temporalizes, it founds time, which implies already carrying its own setting and rising. Unlike the Western psychoanalytic temporality of the subject, which makes time the event's condition of appearance, with Èṣù, temporality is not constituted, it is a constituent; that is, a dimension of experience that invents time through the articulation of events ruled by the origin, that is, by a proto-event that generates a common destiny for all, rendering even the nonexistent visible. In this dimension, the individual is both behind and ahead of themselves. . . . The event that Èṣù inaugurates is not something that can be placed as a mishap in a (hi)story with a given past, present, and future, because he himself makes the (hi)story of his group, therefore, he makes his own time . . . the time of reversibility. In clearer terms, Èṣù's action is not found within time; it invents it.[17]

In this religious and philosophical conception of the genesis and the spiral production of knowledge, the crossroads is a principle of theoretical and metaphysical construction, a semantic operator driven by significance, ostensibly disseminated in Nago-based Brazilian cultural and religious expressions and in those infused by Bantu wisdoms. In Reinados,[18] for example, groups of Congos cross the crossroads with forward and backward movements, retractions, and expansions, in choreographed half-moons. The Moçambiques, on the other hand, walk backward through the crossroads, enhancing the meanings of counterclockwise turns or *giras* in respect to the masters and deities of doors, gates, and crossings, of cartographies and cosmograms of sacredness.[19]

These crossroads of wisdoms and their derived knowledge reveal and teach us the complex, sophisticated, and refined formulations by which memory reinscribes itself, permeates, and restores cultural values of varying range, significance, and rhizomatic expansion.

ANCESTRALITIES, THE SACREDNESS OF EXISTENCE

The sacredness of beings is around all thought implemented by the cognitive systems that infuse the cosmoperception of ancestrality. According to Fu-Kiau, "We are 'sacred' because our natural world is sacred. Our dwellings and our belongings are sacred, because they are made of raw materials taken from the natural world, from the sacred world."[20] In this worldview, the natural world is a reflection of "the greatness of Kalunga," the one who is the "superior energy of life, the one who is entirely complete (*lunga*) by themself."[21]

> In the eyes of African people, especially those in contact with the teachings of ancient African schools, the earth, our planet, is *futu dia n'kisi diakânga Kalûnga mu diâmbu dia môyo*—a sachet (parcel) of medicines tied up by Kalûnga for life on earth. This *futu* or *fûnda* contains everything that life needs for its survival: medicines (*n'kisi / bilôngo*), "food" (*madia*), "drink" (*ndwînu*).[22]

> The natural world for the Bantu people is the totality of totalities tied together like a sachet (*futu*) by Kalûnga, the supreme and most complete energy, within and around everything in the universe (*luya-lungunu*). . . . Thus, when a Mûntu (human being) sees a tiny crystal (*ngêngele*), they see in it not merely its sacredness but also the divine presence of Kalûnga.

> In addition to the attention and admiration given to mountains, valleys, the wind, the sky, and the changes in the natural cycle, the Mûntu pays special attention to the world of the forest because, as it is said, *Mfinda Kasuka tufukidi*—we perish if the forests are extinct. Due to this popular view among the Bantu, the very act of entering the forest becomes a sacred ritual.[23]

The peoples of the African diasporas inherit this perception that the world contains the sacredness of existence and of the diverse beings that compose it, because the vital energy and strength of àṣẹ vibrates in everything. The Nago-Yoruba tradition also embraces a similar cosmoperception. According to Eduardo Oliveira, this vision presides over the entire conception of African-based religions, marked "by exemplary profound sacredness and secular skill. The entire universe is inserted within a religious dynamic. It embraces all domains of life-production, culture, private life, public life, etc. . . . and its goal is to maintain the well-being of the community. It is life for the sake of religion and religion for the sake of life continuity."[24] In the rich *sophyas* supported by African peoples' thought, the notions of person, collectivity, world, nature, cosmos, and their entwinements in the complex universe of ancestrality and sacredness, are essential elements of comprehension. In the Bantu languages, the root word *ntu* unfolds in a rich vocabulary that evokes a thinking consciousness connected to the deities, to the ancestors, to all nature, and to the sacredness that infuses everything. The term *muntu* designates the person, the consciousness of creative thinking. According to Fu-Kiau, the *muntu* (person), is "a system of systems, the pattern of patterns in being."[25] *Bantu*, the plural of *muntu*, designates plural collectivity and its relations with the person. Temporal experience circulates through the *muntu* and the *bantu*, determining all articulations and actions in their surroundings. The *muntu* is the gourd-head, as is the *ori*, from the Nago-Yoruba perspective, a system of vibrations that resonates vital energy. The Bantu worldview connects the *muntu* to the earth, *nsi* (*n'toto*), to everything and everyone that inhabits and exists in it, and to the universe (*nza*), postulating the importance of welcoming the diversity of beings, as highlighted by this beautiful proverb: "A forest of one type of trees is not a forest, it is a '*n'dima*' [orchard] no matter how large it is, for a forest is always an ensemble in diversity."[26]

Henrique Cunha Júnior summarizes this sophisticated and complex *sophya*. According to him,

> *NTU*, [is] the principle of existence of everything. In the African philosophical *Bantu* root, *NTU* designates the essential part of everything that exists and everything that is known through existence. *Muntu* is the person, constituted by the body, mind, culture, and mainly, by the word. The word as a guiding thread of their own history, of their own knowledge of existence. The people, the community, is expressed by the word *Bantu*. . . . *Ubuntu* expresses existence defined by the existence of other existences. I, we, exist because you and others exist; it carries a collaborative sense of collective human existence. . . . The organization of the *Bantu* languages reflects the organization of a philosophy of the human being, of human collectivity and the relationship of these beings with nature and the universe. . . . The knowledge

of reality, and the reflective imagination around the understandings of the consequences of the relationships established between animate and inanimate (in African societies everything is alive) beings of nature, is part of the African philosophies from societies connected to matters of ancestrality, territorial identity, and the transmission of knowledge through words spoken both by human beings and drums.... They are philosophical ways of reflecting, teaching, and learning about the relationships between beings from nature, the cosmos, and human existence.[27]

The spiral conception of time is based on the privileged place of the ancestor who, as Presence, presides over the spirals of time, underwriting transient temporality, the unlimited past, composed per se of accumulated present, past, and future. In Brazil, Kalunga is also known as Ocean Sea, the place of the sacred, mirroring the divinity in which dwells the power of life, death, and crossings. In these interfaces and alliances between the person (*muntu*), the collectivity (*bantu*), and the ancestors, everything pulsates as inseparable and complementary components of the same significant chain, forged by ancestrality, the core, organizing, driving principle, the structure and network of all thought. The Kalunga pot, as it is known, is the core of vital energy in motion. Ancestrality, the agency of *sophya*, initiates *kinesis* in all its realms and competences, the philosophy, conception, and experience of curvilinear temporalities, managing all the creation processes of cultural practices.

Ancestrality structurally defines Black-African cosmoperception, dispersed across its countless and diverse cultures. As Oliveira summarizes, from "the complementarity of genres to the collective character of African rituals, the practice of worshiping ancestors preserves and updates, in the best possible ways, the originality and genuineness of the elements that structure African worldviews," which takes into account "the conception of the universe, of power, of person."[28]

This great principle orders social relations; religious, metaphysical, and secular dimensions; production dynamics; ethical and aesthetic values, measures and exchanges; connections and interdependence between all entities and beings in the cosmos; communication with deities; the junction of principles of generic and individual existence; the necessary alliance between life and death; and the distribution of vital energy; ultimately, everything is ordered and structured inside the ancestral conception, the foundation of civilizational folds.

The philosophical principle of ancestrality is the driving force of the individual body, of the collective body, of the cultural corpus, and of all thought about the human condition, of all ethical and aesthetic plumage, of all knowledge production of all areas, from the most technical to the most transcendental or quotidian, because it takes into account the masculine, feminine, and collective principles in a complementary relationship; because it restores the vital force to its descendants, both those linked by blood ties and those brought together by other kinds of family relationships, grouped by imaginary and symbolic networks of belonging; and because it circumscribes the spiral experience of temporalities and space.

The transformations of this foundational principle are lived and conceived within the family realm, in a concrete and materially figured manner, toward its transcreation and transfamiliar extension in the Americas—particularly in Brazil. This happens as a way of readjusting the principle itself or the subjects circumscribed or associated with it. Within the African diasporic communities in the Americas, the consequent expansion of the concepts of family, kinship and belonging—both in the past and in the present—happened as a form of restitution and reconfiguration of the apprehended and lived principle of ancestrality, during and after slavery. From the engendering of new bonds comes the constitution of a broader family lineage, affectively and symbolically, bringing together the African persons and their descendants in communities of belonging and mutual support, performed in the realm of *casas de Candomblé* or *terreiros*,[29] and in the celebrations of Reinados, for example, as well as in countless other ways of recomposing African heritage and memory.

Ancestrality can be conceived both as a philosophical principle of the African civilizational thought, and as a channel, that is, a means by which the vital force —the generator and storage of dynamic energy, the original sacred *kinesis*—is spread throughout the cosmos, in a never-ending process of expansion and catalysis. For many intellectuals, including Thompson and Fu-Kiau, the idea of a vital force establishes the Bantu *sophya* and, as Aguessy reiterates, in Africa, "different levels of existence and different beings are unified by the 'life force.'" These beings are "the supreme being, the various supernatural beings (gods and spirits), the souls of the dead (ancestors), living men, the vegetable, mineral and animal realm, the realm of magic."[30]

According to Fábio Leite, the vital force that spreads from creation constitutes a principle of universality that "establishes individualizations hierarchized by species, making nature populate itself with forces connected to its most varied domains." Vital force unfolds and multiplies itself, providing "vitality to all beings in the universe" who dwell in it and maintain—positive or negative— exchanges with each other.[31] Still according to Leite, as a principle of the sacredness embedded in all creation, vital energy "is both an abstract category that is amplified in everything that exists and a power that materializes in the most ordinary quotidian relationships, in sociopolitical organizations as well as "within historical practices and practices that explain reality."[32] Oliveira states that, for "the Bantu peoples, the ultimate reality of things is the 'vital force' that animates life. It is life itself. This is why the primary touchstone and the supreme value is the 'vital force.' Thus, the fundamental imperative of Bantu philosophy is the categorical assertion that 'every being is force.'"[33]

According to Laura Padilha, the vital force "constitutes the essence of a view that theorists of African cultures call the Black-African view of the world. Such force makes the living, the dead, the natural and the supernatural, the cosmic and the social elements interact, forming the components of a same indissoluble significant chain.... The ancestors—that is, the predecessors—mediate the living and the dead, as well as the natural and the sacred forces.... They are thus simultaneously close to human beings, to gods, and to the supreme being, whose languages they master."[34] According to Luz, the absorption and transmission of vital force and energy—*àṣẹ* in the Yoruba perspective—are the foundation of the African *ethos* and *arkhé*, which manifest in African-based religions and systems.

> The *arkhé*, however, is not restricted to a social-historical and cultural inaugural principle, but rather it encompasses the mystical energy that constitutes the ancestrality and the cosmic forces that rule the universe in the dynamic interaction of *àṣẹ* restitution in the *áiyé* and in the *orun*, i.e., in this world and beyond and vice versa.
>
> If the ritual characterizes an *ethos*, that is, the aspect of language, style, or form of communication and expression of aesthetic and ethical values and contents of knowing or not knowing, what it performs and animates above all is the restitution and transmission of *àṣẹ*.
>
> The ethos found in the relationships established with the materials, substances, and significant forms in leaf-based preparations, baths and drinks, cooking, *ileke* [sacred beaded necklaces], colors, belts, clothing, gestures, music, dance, poetry, living minds and bodies, constituted in semantic codes, in language; is characterized by expressing and communicating the mobilization of a latent force, an "eidos," found in the concept of *àṣẹ*, the power of realization.[35]

As Luz summarizes, the Black *arkhé* "refers to the inaugural principles," to what translates and instills meaning, strength, and power of realization to the subject and their collectivity. The *arkhé* is also "what makes itself known."[36] According to Sodré, for the Bantu peoples, *muntu* (person) is also "the force of knowing," "'*udi na Buninga bwa kuyuka*,' in the Kiluba language." In both Bantu and

Yoruba cosmologies, "effective knowledge" depends on the absorption of "vital force" and *àṣẹ*, respectively."[37]

Ancestrality is the core principle and the great foundation that shapes all the circulation of vital energy. Religious and secular rituals of African descent reterritorialize ancestrality and vital force as driving principles and agents that infuse Brazilian culture and—in particular—African diasporic artistic-cultural practices, whether in healing medicinal wisdoms; in the production of fabrics and utensils; in architectural forms; in narrative and poetic textures; in dances, music, sculpture, and mask art; in bodily games; in Maracatu, Jongo, and samba; in capoeira; in religious systems; in models of social organization, in relationships between subjects and between humans and the cosmos, and particularly, in the conception of spiral time.

CHRONOSOPHIES IN SPIRALS

Ancestrality is carved out by curved, recurring, ringed time; spiral time, which returns, reestablishes, and transforms, touching everything. Time is ontologically experienced as continuous and simultaneous movements of feedback; anticipation and reversibilities; dilatation; expansion and containment; contraction and relaxation; a synchronicity of instances composed of present, past, and future. It is through ancestrality that the vital force—generator of the universe, one of its gifts—blooms. According to Oliveira:

> African time is impregnated by Vital Force. It is sacred time (*zamani*) that involves the lived time (*sasa*). The past is privileged, for it is the ancestors' time. The past, therefore, is not crystallized. It is potentially transformative, such as the accumulation-tradition of elapsed time. African time, such as the African universe, is pregnant with ancestrality. Just as the visible is not separable from the invisible ... the time of the dead is not separated from the time of the living. . . . This universe and this time are not empty. Besides being permeated by the Vital Force (an attribute of the sacred) and by the harmonious presence of the ancestors (who live in a transcendental dimension), in their insides, time and the universe embrace the person.[38]

The person is the materiality of what prevails in current temporality, underwritten by the past, the present, and by a likely future, a *being* and a system touched by ancestral ontology. This ontological complexity, in which time spins backward and forward, constituting the present, is also postulated by Kenyan philosopher John S. Mbiti. To him, temporal dimensions derive from an ontology. In order to avoid mental associations with the words present, past, and future, Mbiti employs two Swahili words: *Sasa* and *Zamani*, which he interprets as two terms that translate and constitute the conception and perception of temporalities:

> *Sasa* has the sense of immediacy, nearness, and "now-ness"; and is the period of immediate concern for the people, since that is "where" or "when" they exist.... *Sasa* is the time region in which people are conscious of their existence, and within which they project themselves both into the short future and mainly into the past (*Zamani*). *Sasa* is in itself a complete or full time dimension, with its own short future, a dynamic present, and an experienced past. We might call it the Micro-Time (Little Time).... *Zamani* is not limited to what in English is called the past. It also has its own "past," "present" and "future," but on a wider scale. We might call it the Macro-Time (Big Time). *Zamani* overlaps with *Sasa* and the two are not separable. *Sasa* feeds or disappears into *Zamani*. But before events become incorporated into the *Zamani*, they have to become realized or actualized within the *Sasa* dimension. When this has taken place, then the events "move" backward from the *Sasa* into the *Zamani*...the final storehouse for all phenomena and events, the ocean of time in which everything becomes absorbed into a reality that is neither after nor before.... *Sasa* generally binds individuals and their immediate environment together. It is the period of conscious living. On the other hand, *Zamani* is the period of the myth, giving a sense of foundation or "security" to the *Sasa* period; and binding together all created things, so that all things are embraced within the Macro-Time.[39]

In the ancestral African conception, ontology, a channel of vital force, includes, in the same phenomenological circuit, the deities, cosmic nature, fauna, flora, physical elements, the dead, the living, and those who are yet to be born, conceived as bonds of a necessary complementarity, in a continuous process of transformation and becoming. This cosmic and philosophical perception interweaves time, ancestrality, and death in the same circuit of significance. That is why burial rituals stand out in the realm of African descent. Roach, for example, pays special attention to the funerals of Black people in New Orleans.[40] In Brazil, whether within Jeje-based, Nago-based, or Bantu-based religions such as the Reinados, burial rituals are emblematic as acts of retraction and expansion of the driving force and as environments where ancestrality is enacted.

Such as the word, death is an event, a necessary act in the dynamics of transformation and renewal of everything that exists, allowing the continuous movements of the cosmos and its permanent renewal and revitalization. If, in the familiar plan, death means the loss of the individual, in the collective plan, it means their enrichment. Thus, the importance of the funeral rituals, which act as forces restoring the balance momentarily broken, a way of mastering death, the gaps and the voids, a balance once restored by the performances of the funeral ceremonies, which, "if, on the one hand, they can be considered as rites of passage, on the other hand, they also constitute rituals of permanence, for the ancestors are born from them."[41]

According to Júlio Braga, "the funeral ritual dignifies the dead person as an element that is inseparable from the religious structure and from the very sense of permanence and elaboration of the power transference system that passes the power on to the new leader who takes over the direction of a religious group."[42] Thus, the funeral ritual becomes one of the most fruitful transfer channels of energy and vital force from the individual to the collectivity, interweaving life and death in the same kinesthetic spirals of concentration and distribution, permanence and ephemerality.

One of the most pungent, beautiful, and important funeral ceremonies in Reinados is called *Descoroação dos Reis e dos Grandes Mestres* (Dethronement of Kings and Great Masters), a rite of passage, one of the stages of transformation of a person into a celebrated and revered ancestor whose energy spreads out to the living, fertilizing existence with the energies of vital forces. The ancestor is waves and radiations, memory archives, an accumulation of temporalities. The ancestors are "the biological, material, intellectual and spiritual treasures accumulated in scrolls [*ku mpèmba*], the past, i.e., the perpetual bank of the generating/ driving forces of life. . . . There is no end in the dingo-dingo process, the perpetual going-and-coming-back of life as well as in the Mûntu's [*mwèla-ngîndu*]. Life is a continuum through many stages. For the Bântu, there is no death and no resurrection; for them life is a continual process of change."[43] In this *ciranda*,[44] there are interval-gaps, moments for crying or smiling, but these moments are not the ultimate and final horizon, nor the climax of a found becoming, or a past tense apart from the present, for, in this system of thought, there is no absolute end as in the end of times, as "there is no static enclosure of the subject, held in the repetitions of mechanical or stagnant cyclic returns."[45] Death, the good death, integrates the possibility of life, a continuum. In this continuum, "the process of living (being, appearing, coming into being in the natural world) and dying (leaving, disconnecting from the natural world)—that is, igniting

FIGURE 2.2. Jota Mombaça, *Your blood is land where no one steps* (film still, 2024. 18:45). Photo: Lu Peixe.

and extinguishing, turning on and off"—are interconnected. "One cannot exist without the other. Our natural world is sacred because it carries both life and death in perfect balance to keep all existence in it in movement. To destroy this balance and its sacredness is to cause an end to it and to all of us."[46]

Being able to be in ancestrality is being able to be in the sacredness of everything that involves us. Black cultures are mirrored in these knowledges that circulate and manifest themselves through a prism of formulations and forms that guide *oralituras*, their means and modes of veridiction, their force of permanence and Presence.

BETWEEN ETHICS AND AESTHETICS, OFFERINGS

Cultural practices in which the body—the subject's living body—is the favored agent allow us to state that all art, and every performance, translates a meaningful style that distinguishes culture and the people who bring it to life and respond to philosophical and cognitive languages and to a plethora of aesthetic references and complex stylization modes. If we think of a particular style of composition and being, we can conclude with Murray that "the creation of an art style is . . . a major cultural achievement. In fact, it is perhaps the highest as well as the most comprehensive fulfillment of culture; for an art style, after all, reflects nothing so much as the ultimate synthesis and refinement of a lifestyle."[47]

As a cultural style, performances embody and illustrate values. They are a mode of apprehension and interpretation of the world and a means of permanence and belonging for individuals who take part in them. When it comes to ritual performances, we can also enjoy the elaboration of their poetics, set by voice inflections, by the edges of the moving body and the poetics of its gestures. Here, ancestrality vibrates and restores, performing the repertoire of our *africanias*, both the oldest and the most recent ones, which improvise with and germinate in their predecessors.[48]

Underlining basic African and African diasporic concepts and forms of organization does not mean expressing an essentialist ideal of tradition, in which tradition is thought as a storage of materials and sensorial stimuli or as a museological repertoire from which culture and its subjects pick and choose the elements that translate their origin or identity. It means highlighting the stylistic processes of refiguration and metamorphosis that were and are derived from all transcultural signifying and cognitive crossings, in which signs and their significance appear in a state of transit(ion)—thus, in transformation, including in terms of aesthetics. The very comprehension of art, its nature and apprehension, already places some questions and aporias. What is called *art* is not always the same in different cultures and societies; in many of them, the very concept (of art) is not favored, so there are not rigid differentiations between *craft* and *art*, and beauty—or the idea of beauty—is not exclusively associated with specific practices or platforms, expressing hierarchies of concepts and values. Therefore, aesthetic values are also ethical values.

This perspective allows us to affirm that, in many cultures, including African cultures and cultures of African descent, aesthetic production evokes patterns, modes, conventions, and stylizations, and the cosmologies that ground them. Thinking alongside Murray, we can affirm that no art is non-aesthetic, because every artistic expression, simple as it may seem, exists and comes to be through refined stylistic modes and conventions:

> Esthetic problems are not likely to require less esthetic insight and orientation simply because the subject matter at hand happens to be black experience. Certainly, no artist can accept the suggestion that art is artless. Not even the most spontaneous-seeming folk expression is artless. No matter how crude some folk music, for example, might sound to the uninitiated, its very existence depends on a highly *conventionalized* form. Folk airs, ditties, tunes and ballads are labeled traditional precisely because they conform to well-established even if unwritten principles of composition and formal structure peculiar to a given genre or idiom

which, after all, is an esthetic *system* in every essential or functional meaning of the phrase.[49]

In many cultures and societies, aesthetic enjoyment is not separate from functionality in their singing and dancing, their craftsmanship, sculptures, symbolic representations, sciences, music, hairstyles, architecture, rites, and delicacies. This does not mean they require less attention or that they do not demand critical-historical perspectives in order to be approached and valued. The Yoruba people, for instance, "accesses everything aesthetically—from the flavor and color of a yam to the characteristics of a pigment, the clothing and conduct of a man or a woman."[50] According to Tiganá Santana: "To many Black civilizations, aesthetics is not an accessory or a posterior sense.... Aesthetics is a dimension that translates ancestral aesthetics of being, in other words, the lines on a fabric, an *oriki* (sacred poem from the Yoruba universe in the African continent), a string instrument from Mali, a mask, a gesture of realization, or the geometry of food in a recipient translate the *Kalunga*'s proposition."[51] However, there is a fundamental ethical comprehension, found in all kinds of making, which is aggregated to and indissociable from aesthetic pleasure. In other words, the aesthetic is not perceived as separate from its ethical dimension. As Cunha Jr. teaches us, in all the African-based cultural expressions, there is the ethical component as the organizer of the cognitive system, which expresses itself in modalities "of generally known collective philosophy, producing ethical values that regulate the daily lives of African societies which are deemed traditional (tradition here means the repetition in time, with changes and innovations, but always referring to a history of the past and passed on through a normative social ritual)."[52]

One of the ethical values found in Black cultures is that cultural goods are ultimately radio transmitters of the vital energy that spreads from what is sacred and manifests itself in everything. It requires listening and attention. As Thompson summarizes, in many African cultures "the radiance of the eyes, the magnification of the gaze, reflects *àṣẹ*, the brightness of the spirit."[53] In all of its manifestations and iterations, artistic expression becomes a noble quality when, in its powerful functionality, it reverberates this brightness of the spirit, the act of doing good for the collective well-being to tend to the need of social balance, a posture and a postulate of the ethics and *sophya* that inform them.

Within this thought, beauty is never uninterested or intermittent. In order to be beautiful, something must necessarily be a benefit from and for the collective. Aesthetics, as a translation and a transmitter of *sophya*, is that which is ethical. It is not exalted as an attribute to be priced, but rather as a derivation of its value to the social collective, a usufruct. As Jones reports:

If we think of African music as regards its intent, we must see that it differed from Western music in that it was a purely *functional* music. Borneman lists some basic types of songs common to West African cultures: songs used by young men to influence young women (courtship, challenge, scorn); songs used by older men to prepare the adolescent boys for manhood, and so on.... It was, and is, inconceivable in the African culture to make a separation between music, dancing, song, the artifact, and a man's life or his worship of his gods. *Expression* issued from life, and *was* beauty. But in the West, "the triumph of the economic mind over the imaginative," as Brooks Adams said, made possible this dreadful split between life and art. Hence, a music that is an "art" music as distinguished from something someone would whistle tilling a field.[54]

In this perspective, according to Cunha Jr., African thought and cosmoperception are expressed as philosophy through "ways of thinking, taken from myths, proverbs, and the social commitments that constitute a social ethics, which reflects, inscribes (and even writes)... recording, in orality, the contingencies of human existence, social formation, power and justice relations, life's continuity." Their functionality and adequacy determine their value as a good that comes from and works toward the balance of the community, for they are "pragmatic philosophies for solving the problems of life on Earth, deeply linked to the existence and the balance of the forces of healthy continuity of these existences, in the dynamics of the conflicts and possibilities of balance."[55]

For Mestre Didi, the ethics of culture presupposes some commitments. According to him, the willingness to innovate in the arts must be integrated with cultural values: "This articulation can only happen successfully when the author, in addition to having technical sensibility, is deeply committed to their tradition. When their technique is at the service of the cosmic knowledge and initiative of their culture, to which they are heir and transmitter, only then their innovations will have authentic unfoldings and expansions."[56] In the practices of making, even when an author does not relinquish the recognition of individual authorship, their name is not necessarily the only one that must be recognized: "Africa did have, as it does today, its own 'masters of thought' because their ideas remain with us: proverbs, legends, tales, myths, etc., even though their names are not known, because names are not very important in the African concept in the process of art creation. No one creates alone."[57] The call and response technique, as well as all the modulations and African-nuanced performative forms—prioritize the circumlocution that includes everyone in the very act of making (something) happen. And they translate a meaningful style that distinguishes culture and the people who bring it to life and respond to philosophical and cognitive languages and to a plethora of aesthetic references and complex stylization modes. As a cultural style, these practices embody and illustrate values; they are a way of apprehending and interpreting the world, as well as a means of permanence and belonging for the individuals circumscribed by them in the desired pleasure of being, existing, resonating, giving, and radiating.

Art is thus a gift and an offering.

POETICS
OF *ORALITURA*

Não há lugar achado
sem lugar perdido.
Casam-se além as falas de um lugar,
no encontro da memória
com a matriz.

[There is no place found
without a place lost.
The tongues of a place unite beyond,
in the meeting of memory
with the origin.]
— RUY DUARTE DE CARVALHO, *Hábito da terra*

POIESIS OF THE CANVAS-BODY

In the compositions that follow, I intend to work out some *gestas* through which spiral time, as a structure, manifests itself.[1] I seek to investigate its language; its productions and recorded images; the kinesthetic exploration of the body; its functions as a device and as the conductor, portal, and canvas of *graphyas* and of a syntax of adornments; its spatial expansions and the scansions of its duration; its perception as deixis; its memories of Africa. The feats of spiral time I address

FIGURE 3.1. Val Costa, *Untitled I*, from the series *Precious*, 2024. In each canvas there is an inscription: "It is not taboo to turn back / and recover everything that was taken from us."

here are translated by poetics that are nuanced and influenced by a constitutive embodied practice expressed by the canvas-body.

The canvas-body is an image-body.

Usually, we address images visually, favoring the gaze, our eyes, the window to the soul, as evoked by the ancient Greeks. But images can also contain sound and movement, and both of these qualities are contiguous. The invitation to see is preceded by the invitation to listen in many of the aesthetic and creative endeavors mentioned here, as they also reveal the formation and recording of images, but these are images that present themselves to our eyes and to our listening. This interdependence is important and invites not only the expansion of our eyes, but also the expansion of our hearing, along with all our sensory perception, since listening to images is one of the gateways to this universe where movements, sounds, luminosity, and aromas have colors and draw landscapes of knowledge, a privileged realm of *oralituras*.

The canvas-body, as material and mental image, background, surface, volume, terrain, perspective, and condensation, does not refer only to body paintings, body accessories, and adornments, and, consequently, the favoring of visibility poetics; as a sonority, it also evokes auditory evidence, the scrutiny of hearing, the intense activation of auricular registers. In its iconic and visual quality, it provokes the gaze, for the "experience of the image, prior to the experience of the word, takes root in the body," as Bosi states.[2] But the image is not limited to nor resides only in its iconic quality and pictorial attraction, it is not just an icon of the subject or object "fixed on the retina," because it expands as a mental image, in which the "act of seeing captures not only the object's appearance, but some relationship between us and that appearance," as Bosi argues.[3] And he goes on, stating that sounds and words, as expression, "still carry marks, traces, or *echoes* from a deeper relationship between the body of the person who speaks and the world they speak about."[4] And the image, as a sign, is marked, "in all its laborious gestation, by the excavation of the body."[5]

The canvas-body as an image-body presents itself also as a mental image, bringing together the appearance of the being and its vibrations, carrying and postulating thoughts. As Samain warns us, images are thinking forms. As such, they convey thoughts that affect us in various ways and whose reception and perception have the power to also affect and prolong, over time, images and their adherence, because "every image (a drawing, a painting, a sculpture, a photograph, a film frame, an electronic or infographic image) *offers us something to think about*: sometimes a piece of *reality* to gnaw at, *sometimes* a spark of *imagination* to dream about."[6] According to the same author, "every image is a memory of memories," that is, a sort of "survival" that, by combining "a set of signifying data (traits, colors, movements, emptiness, terrains, and many other sensitive and sensory punctuations)," constitutes "a thinking form" that, when associated—just as verbal or musical phrases—are "capable of sparking and promoting 'ideas' or 'ideations'; that is, *movements of ideas*."[7]

Composed of condensations, volume, topography, and perspectives, surface, background, and layers, intensities, and densities, the canvas-body is an image-body, constituted by a complex entwinement of articulations that interlace and intertwine, undulating with their surroundings, imbued with gestures and sounds, wearing and composing codes and systems. The canvas-body encompasses movements, sonorities, and vocalities, choreographies, gestures, language, costumes, pigments or pigmentations, body paintings and hair designs, adornments and accessories, graphisms and graffiti, lights and chromatisms, which stylistically graph this body/corpus as a locus and environment of wisdom and memory. Therefore, it is kinesis, kinesthetic impulse, a significant condensation, a performative synthesis par excellence, in all the wide range of its nature, as a habit, conduct, lexicon, and ideogram. A body, the poetic synthesis of movement. A hieroglyphic body.

Physically, expressively, and perceptively, this complex, porous body, invested with multiple meanings and dispositions, is the place and environment for the inscription of *graphyas* of knowledge, it is device and conductor, a portal and web of memory and performative languages framed by an ingenious syntax of compositions.

Carved out by discontinuities, reversibilities, temporalizing *giras*, sound and rhythmic waves, the embodied event includes individual and collective experiences, personal memory, and social-historical memory. The canvas-body is thus also a cultural corpus which, within its distinct realm, adherences, and multiple profiles, becomes a locus and a privileged environment for countless poetics intertwined in aesthetic making. A body historically implied by a pulsating language that, in its circuits of resonances, inscribes the utterer-emissary subject, their surroundings and ambiences, in a specific circuit of expression, potency, and power.

In their countless modes of realization, in their poetics and aesthetic landscapes, Black embodied practices, as theoretical, conceptual, and performative foundations, as an epistemic system, fecundate events, expanding the canvas-body's connections, like stained-glass windows, radiating and reflecting experiences, existences, desires, as well as our memory perceptions and operations. A thought-body. And also a body of affections.

DANCING THE TIME, DANCER INSCRIPTIONS

In time, the body dances.[8] Robert Farris Thompson states that Africa introduces a new art history, a history of danced art, which specifically and uniquely finds its exponential vehicle of veridiction and stylization in the body.[9] Fu-Kiau also refers to Africa as a "dancing continent," where prevails a powerful trio, drumming-singing-dancing, through which chants of peace, inner strength, and power are created, and in which music "is the expression of life, peace, and harmony."[10] "Kongo people drum, sing, and dance to raise their families with the balance provided by the sound of music. They drum, sing, and dance to mourn their dead; they drum, sing, and dance to strengthen their institutions. Furthermore, [they] drum, sing, and dance because life itself is a perpetual melody. They produce music and enjoy it to be [at] peace with themselves . . . nature, and with the universe as well. Drumming, singing, and dancing is a powerful spiritual 'medicin/n'kisi.'"[11] In Kikongo, one of Congo's Bantu languages, the same verb, *tanga*, refers to the acts of writing and dancing. From its root word derives also the term *ntangu*, one of the designations of time, a polysemic correlation.[12] Here, in a choreography of returns, dancing means inscribing curvilinear temporalities into time and as time. Therefore, the ritual performance is, simultaneously, a line, a trace, a twist, a recurring time, and an act of inscription, an *afrografia*.[13]

In this rhythmic grammar, there are advances and retreats, progression and retroaction, expansion and condensation, in a simultaneous temporal contraction and dilation that determine the spatialities also as drawn, choreographed, cartographed *giras*. On this matter, Graziela Rodrigues states:

> The meaning of opening the Rosary, in *Congado*, or opening an Umbanda *gira*, is directly related to specific points of space that keep and receive the memory of those who perform the rite. Such opening also represents the possibility of making spaces more dynamic, involving interior and exterior movement integrated into the smallest actions. Thus the conversion of everyday spaces into sacred spaces takes place, for the arrangement of such spaces is related to how long people must stay there, so the ancestors' memory can be reinstated in the present. In the same place where it is opened, the Rosary, the *Gira*, the *Giro*, or the *Roda* [Circle] is also closed. In the act of closing, the present time is well located and the future of new festivities is projected and kept in the enigmatic space-time symbolized by the altar or the *conga*. . . . The spaces are present in people's bodies through an interconnection sewn by ritual acts.[14]

Up and down, backward and forward, in every direction, the body sculpts the bonds of ancestrality. The dancer's body is both a ground-body, the earth where the ancestral roots, the ancestor's heart, pulsates as drum beats, and also, rising toward infinity, a pole-body, as the same author beautifully describes it:

> Drawing from an intense relationship with the earth, the body prepares itself for dancing. The feet's capacity of penetrating into the ground, establishing a deep contact, allows the body's entire physical structure to be ideated from its base. According to the image we have of alignment, every structure has roots. . . . Through the parallel position of one's feet, one's entire bone structure and one's musculature is aligned, following its own design, in a spiral. . . . The structure absorbs the symbolism of the offering pole, enunciated by the banner that represents the saints of devotion. The lower part of the pole connects to the earth and the upper part connects to the sky. . . . The upper part of the pole-body is symbolized by the banner, mobilizing the ethereal space around and beyond itself. . . . Arms and hands interact in the construction of the pole and the flag, animating the energies above. . . . The pole-body is firm and flexible, articulated in all directions, integrating inside and outside, up and down, front and back.[15]

This whole pendular process between tradition and its transmission implements a curvilinear, reactivating, and prospective movement that synchronically integrates the present of the past and the future in the moment of the performed act. In the Moçambiques' dances, for example, the rhythm is given by one's shoulder blades, as they expand over the torso, which, in turn, bends toward the lower parts of the body, finding the flow of one's feet. In samba, this shoulder and torso movement weaves the hips into spirals, into *rebolejo*.[16]

In these choreographies, the gesture syncopates from top to bottom, sideways, and in a myriad of directions. The body is thrown downward in a sudden movement, interrupting the linear flow, creating what is called *ginga*.[17] According to Sodré, "the syncopation, the missing beat," "is the absence of a (weak) beat in the bar which, in turn, reverberates into a stronger one. . . . In fact, both in jazz and in samba, syncopation plays a special role, inciting the listener to fill in the missing beat with something to mark time—clapping, nodding, swaying, dancing. The body is also missing—in the appeal of syncopation. Its magnetic force . . . comes from the impulse (caused by the rhythmic gap) to complete the missing beat with the dynamics of movement in space."[18] Movement here translates asymmetry, the raw material of Black embodied practice. This is how syncopation manifests itself, the mother of *ginga* and all *giras*, the body that defies the void, the asymmetrical twists of rhythm in the body that seems to fall, attracted to the ground, then jumps and breaks the fall, spinning over itself and toward expanded spatiality. When playing capoeira, the body slides and swings in the air, drawing the space. It slips, but does not fall, as Mestre Pavão teaches us: "If one of the *capoeiristas* [capoeira players] has some imbalance, the *cantador* [singer], for instance, can sing to remind them that capoeira [players] do not fall, they only slip, emphasizing the technique, the skill, the mastery needed for a good performance in the game." In capoeira, according to Pavão, "everything is complementation." In its elements, stands out "the realm of transience, of *autopoiesis*, of embodied practice.... The *roda* [capoeira circle] is a fight but, simultaneously, it is still a dance."[19]

The syncopation of the gesture demands bodily availability; this is an effect of techniques and procedures apprehended through a diverse methodology, recreated in the doing/redoing, which Zeca Ligiéro, echoing Fu-Kiau, defines as "singing, dancing, drumming," naming these actions as "driving forces." Ligiéro describes the movements and gestures of capoeira Angola as follows: "When it comes to capoeira angola, the playful element is directly intertwined with body movement, which involves the simulation of a fight as an attack-and-defense exercise in a technique where the body transfers its weight constantly between arms and legs, creating a bridge across the vertical and the horizontal axis, at times imitating animals, at times creating a new repertoire of old phrases learned from the masters and announced by the orchestra of *berimbaus, atabaques, pandeiros,* and *agogôs.*"[20] Syncopation draws the moving body's circumscriptions, the voice's solfeggios, and the poetics of gestures. Dancing gestures. This is how time is graphed, composed of the body's spinnings and the poetics of its gestures. The gesture, the expression of movement, is a cultural code that socially signifies. Like every sign, in its symbolic status, the gesture, regardless of its nature, is a convention, an interpreting-sign in any semiotic production of a culture, and, by extension, of all cognitive construction processes operated by said culture in the social, aesthetic, and philosophical domains, et cetera.

In the realm of Black ritual performances, the gesture, besides its so-called exterior, descriptive, illustrative, and even expressive functions, can and should be thought of as an interior and anterior "in itself," a significant condensation, a performative synthesis par excellence, in all the extensive range of its nature, as a habit, a conduct, a lexicon, an ideogram, and a hieroglyph. For Paul Zumthor, as well as for Artaud and Meyerhold, gestures of the face (expression and mime), gestures of the upper limbs, gestures of the head, gestures of the torso, and gestures of the entire body, when together, "carry meaning in the form of hieroglyphic writing."[21]

Gestures, according to Galard, are "the poetry of the act."[22] In verbal poetry, "vowels and consonants rediscover their flavor, their perfume, their tactile quality, while the alphabetic characters release all the symbolism of their graphism."[23] Gestures (distinct from mere gesturing) find their best translation in their poetic function. Thus, poetry, "instead of being primarily a collection of (verbal) objects," is perhaps a process with enough autonomy to operate "similarly, in the construction of words, in the arrangement of objects, in the composition of gestures."[24] Therefore, thinking along with Galard, that "the poetic operation consists of some functioning of signs (rather than the use of some signs)," we can assert that "poetry, whether verbal or gestural, reanimates extinct signs, so that all prose becomes more alive."[25]

Also for Paul Zumthor, the relationships between gesture, movement, and dance with poetry and drama are ostensible and essential: "However the social group orients or limits it, the function of gesture in performance manifests the primary connection between the human body and poetry. . . . Gesture generates in space the external form of the poem. It founds its temporal unity, splitting it from its recurrences. In the griot's monologue, dancing must appear from interval to interval for the narrative to progress."[26] In the realm of *oralituras*, gestures go beyond being merely mimetic representation of a symbolic apparatus conveyed by performance; they also implement and enact performance itself. In other words, gestures are not only narrative or descriptive; they are also fundamentally performative. The gesture, as a *poiesis* of movement and as a minimal form, might evoke the fullest range of senses.

Gestures sculpt the features of memory in space; not its mnemonic trace as a specular copy of the objective reality, but its strength as time in motion. In Africa, as in the Americas, "a good dancer is one who converses with music, clearly hears and feels the beat, and is capable of using different parts of the body to create visualizations of the rhythms."[27] In this perspective, Malone, along with Thompson, concludes that "dancers themselves become a magnificent form of sculptural art." In many traditional African societies, sculptures do not aim to realistically and mimetically portray the body; instead they usually aim to reproduce culturally significant body postures and gestures. Many African sculptors, even in the creation of masks, "seem less interested in precise anatomical representation than in the more subtle processes of implied bodily motion."[28] As asserted by Sodré, in Black culture "the interdependence between music and dance affects the formal structures of both, in such a way that music can be elaborated according to certain dance movements, just as dance can be conceived as a visual dimension of music."[29]

The importance of the gesture when invoking Ògún is described by Graciela Rodrigues as follows: "Ògún, whose hands and arms become spaces 'that cut through trouble and open paths,' touches his left palm with the side of his right hand in the cutting movement . . . corresponding to the solar chakra, associated to this Orisha's realm. Another correspondence is that, in Ògún's warrior dance, the swordlike movement of his hands, before the Orisha projects them into space, develops toward the other plexuses located on the torso and related to his posture."[30] Suzana Martins, sharing this perspective, describes the conquering of spaces installed by Yemoja's dance, in her turns and swings which border and circumscribe spaces:

> At other times, Yemoja Ogunté subtly performs a very common movement also observed in other Orishas' dances: holding her cutlass with her right hand, Yemoja Ogunté stretches her right arm and points it forward, towards the ground, almost touching it; in a quick impulse, with her whole body, she heavily rotates on the axis of her semi-curved spine, with accentuated speed, drawing a circle in space, around her own body. In this quick and abrupt turning movement, the volume of her skirts expands the visual sensation of the space her body occupies, creating the image of a tornado. . . . According to *filha-de-santo*[31] Janail Peixoto (1992), this turn means that "Yemoja Ogunté is circumscribing her space, warning the enemy not to advance."[32]

The body dances time. Dancing is akin to the act of inscribing, which is like being in the curved time of movement. The event created in and by the body inscribes subject and culture in a reflected spatiality, mirroring temporalities. Therefore, we can conceive the ritual performance not only as an inscription of the body in spatialities, but as a projection of space in a temporality that mirrors it. The danced movements mimic this spiral circularity, whether in the body's dancing, or in the spatial occupation that the spinning body draws around itself. The choreographic movement occupies the space in unfolded circles, figuring the excentric notion of time. In other words: time, in its spiral dynamics, can only be conceived through space or in the spatiality of the gap occupied by the moving body. Time and space thus become mutually mirrored images.

In the derivations of *ntu*, a suffix of Bantu languages, the term *hantu*, as a "classificatory category of places," designates spatialities, as well as temporal passages and landscapes: "HANTU is a category that classifies places. In African thought, we understand that a place is defined in relation to time. The space-time category forms a binomial produced by the classification in Hantu. Words linked to the cardinal points, geographic spaces, or map-like descriptions are inside this category, as well as yesterday, today, and tomorrow. Morning, afternoon, evening, night, and dawn. Hantu is the type of energy of spatial location, temporal location, and of the movement of changes."[33] In Black ritual dances, the concave and convex choreographies that create a space of circumscription of the subject and the cosmos lead us not only to the semantic and symbolic universe of the action being re-presented, but constitute the action itself as a temporality. To dance is to perform, to inscribe. Ritual performance is, therefore, an act of inscription, a *graphya*, a bodygraphy.[34] In predominantly oral and gestural cultures, such as African and Indigenous cultures, for instance, the body is, par excellence, the site and environment of memory.

But, in these traditions, the body is not just the illustrative extension of the knowledge dynamically shaped by secular conventions and paradigms. This body/corpus is not only repeating a habit; it is also implementing, interpreting, and revising the re-presented action, event, or happening. Therefore, it is crucial to emphasize the meta-constitutive nature of the body in these traditions, where action is inseparable from reflection, and content is intertwined with form; memory is graphed on the body, serving as a perpetual register that continuously transmits and modifies it.

This peculiar form of expression, relying on the body as its exponential — although not exclusive — vehicle of language, is deeply rooted in the inherent and inseparable relationship between sound, gesture, and bodily movements. It envelops the body with a multitude of knowledges, such as rhythms and vocalities, visually embroidering words, music, and vocalization in the air, instilling a pictorial quality into sonorities, drawing and recording the spirals of time in them.

TIME, RHYTHM OF SONORITIES

Dancing the word, singing the gesture, resonating in every movement a drawing of the voice, a prism of pronunciations, a rhythmic calligraphy, a cadence. This is how the emission of oral textuality takes place, in the manifold devices by and in which it is composed. In the soundscape, many forms not only recreate, in terms of utterance, the historical reminiscence of African peoples in the Americas itself, but also reinvent, transcreate, and inscribe it, as call and response, in techniques and performances of countless genres and diverse supports of creative utterance of poetic language games, reinventing aesthetic knowledge in different pronunciations, phrasings, and poetic veins.

These ingenious, complex, and multiple repertoires, safeguarded in the spirals of memory, vibrant in beautiful songs and tales, performed in multiple vocal and rhythmic timbres, inscribe distinct transits and poetic intersections in the *gra-phya* of the voice and in sound rhizomes, as waves and radiation. This plethora of sonorities is presented from the most extensive *gestas* to the smallest sound cells. It is found in singing, vocalities, percussions, onomatopoeias, whistles, pronunciations, phrasings, solfeggios, vocalizations, as well as in multiple construction processes of sound languages and musicalities, like voice engravings.

According to Juana Elbein, "Words are important as long as they are sound, as long as they are pronounced. The emission of sound is the culmination of a process of internal polarization.... From every formulation of sound, a third element is born as a synthesis.... The sound is the outcome of a dynamic structure, in which the appearance of the third term creates movement. In every system, the number three is associated with movement."[35] This third element, the number three, which evokes movement, can be found in the three *atabaques* of Candomblé and capoeira, this three is in Jongo and Tambores de Minas. It is also found in Batuques, and in the Candombes, as well as in the Reinados' practice. It is a marker of the spiral movement. Around the beat of the three sacred drums gravitate the deities, ancestors, driving forces, sensibility and perception, emotions, offerings, the person, and the entire community.

Drums are rhythm makers. In the texture of their timbres, rhythmic qualities and complexities shine. Rhythms, in turn, enchant sounds. "Sound, whose time is ordered in rhythm, is a crucial element in African cultures," states Sodré.[36] Rhythm is the most distinctive quality of Black *verbivocomusical* (verbal-vocal-musical) creations, and it is graphed, as a synthesis, in the dynamics of major time, in spirals. Let us hear Sodré: "As every rhythm is already a synthesis (of beats), Black rhythm is a synthesis of (sound) syntheses, which attests to the integration of the human element into mythical temporality. Every sound that the human individual emits reaffirms their condition as a singular being, every rhythm to which they adhere leads them to revive a collective wisdom about time, where there is no place for anguish, because what transpires is the overflowing joy of activity, of induced movement."[37] In Black aesthetic formulations, rhythms are also distributed and manifested in the language of percussion instruments, which translate this complex, subtle, and sophisticated sound repercussion. Jones had already observed how, in the beat of the drums, there are rhythmic qualities installed as means and devices of communication, "and not, as was once thought, merely by using the drums in a kind of primitive Morse code, but by the phonetic reproduction of the words themselves —the result being that Africans developed an extremely fine and extremely complex rhythmic sense, and have become unusually responsive to timbral subtleties."[38]

The rhythm of the drums and the percussion of all the instruments echo in the performative reminiscence of the body, making the body resonate the radiances of time itself, in a contiguous expressive syntax that fertilizes the kinship between the living, the ancestors, and those yet to be born, for "African rhythms contain the measure of a homogeneous time (cosmic or mythical temporality) which is capable of continually turning back on itself, where every end is the cyclical restart of a situation."[39] According to Zumthor, the drums "announce the true word, [they] exhale the ancestors' breath."[40]

ON THE SPOKEN WORD

In the performance of *oralituras*, the spoken word as expression is one of the most important transmitters, especially the spoken word as power of speech, which, like mill wheels, is capable of bringing into being what, as sound, can manifest itself as materiality. Materially, words are sound, and, as such, they are part of the structuring synthesis of an entire continent of dilated and embodied sonorities in the dynamics of kinesis. The auratic and numinous quality of words, an original in-itself, simultaneously signified and signifier, reverberates and echoes in percussions and rhythms that incarnate the chants and infuse the body.

In the context of African and African Brazilian cognitive systems, words, besides being signs—in the sense that they represent something—are also invested with effectiveness and power, since the spoken word maintains the effectiveness of not only designating the thing to which it refers, but also carrying in itself the thing-in-itself. It carries in itself what it evokes; as a container, as a force of utterance, it contains that which the voice has named and designated. It is the event in itself. As Zumthor points out, "words uttered by Voice create what they say."[41]

Words hold the power to make happen what they release in their vibration. In words are the deities, the ancestors, the *Nkisi*, the prayers that heal and perform the oracular time of enigmas, the past and becoming, the sounds that emit, transmit, conceal, unveil, dim, or illuminate. In words and in chants, the ancestors are, and so, in words and in chants, time is. Hence the numinous nature and auratic power of the spoken word.

In these linguistic contexts, the word as *oralitura* acquires a unique resonance, investing and inscribing the subject who manifests it or to whom it is addressed in a cycle of expression and power. In the circuit of tradition, which preserves the ancestral words, and in the circuit of transmission, which re-actualizes and moves it into the present, words are wind, breath, pronunciation, event, and performance, markers of wisdom. This wisdom becomes an event not because it is crystallized in memory, but mostly because it is reedited in the performance of the singer/narrator and in the collective response to it. The spoken word exists at the moment of its expression, when it articulates the contiguous syntax through which it is performed, fertilizing the kinship between people, the ancestors, and the deities.

As Zumthor teaches us, the spoken word does not exist "in a purely verbal context: it necessarily participates in a broader process, operating over an existential situation it alters in some way and whose totality engages the bodies of the participants. On the border between two semiotic domains, the *gestus* accounts for the fact that a bodily attitude finds its equivalent in a voice inflection, and vice versa, continuously."[42] As I have already pointed out in *Afrografias da memória*, the spoken word is thus performed as language, knowledge, and enjoyment, because it combines, in its pronunciation and veridiction, music, gesture, dancing, and singing, and also because it needs to be appropriately and adequately performed. It needs to be uttered in certain and specific ways to reach its desired effectiveness.[43] In Reinados, for example, each situation and ritual moment requires appropriate language, which is expressed through chants: There are entrance chants; exit chants; road chants; path/journey chants; chants for hoisting flags; chants for raising flagpoles; chants for saluting, greeting, invoking chants to cross doors, gates, and crossroads; and many others. Thus, in each situation, the soloist emits the suitable chant for that place and moment, since the meaning of words and their power of action depend, to a great extent, on them being appropriately performed. Knowing how to activate the energy of the chant, the vibration of the voice, and the gestural movements is necessary, so the chant can be fully efficient in its production of senses. Performance engenders the possibilities of significance and the effectiveness of ritual language.

Juana Elbein also emphasizes the strength of words and their power of action: "The spoken word has the power of action. . . . If words acquire such power of action, they do so because they are impregnated with *àṣẹ*, pronounced with breath—the existential transmitter—with saliva, with temperature. It is the breathed and lived word, accompanied by modulations, emotional charge, the personal history and the power of the one who utters it."[44] Therefore, words are also power. The one who utters them bears all responsibility for what is said and the voice with which it is said, for the word is also an oracle and an action. Amaral emphasizes this idea: "Among the Vatonga of Inhambane, as in all of traditional Africa, words are spoken, recited, and sung in order to become increasingly effective in their specific function of mediating the past, the present, and the future. For the Vatonga of Inhambane, the spoken word 'is not lost in the air," for it has its own power and always produces a beneficial or harmful effect, depending on the intention, the dignity, and the state of mind of the subject who utters it."[45] The effectiveness of what is said amplifies the voice's powers, because, as a sound figure, "the voice alone warmly instills the trace of the action to come in the existential fabric."[46] Just as in distant Africa, where, "for centuries," everything "within the space of African communal life has been built/destroyed . . . by the effectiveness of the voices which restored the past, advanced the present, and announced the future, before and during the centuries of white-European domination, when writing was not a part of their cultural heritage."[47]

Ritual words fertilize the phenomenological life cycle—the dynamic consensus between human and divine, between the ancestors, the living, the infants, and those who are yet to be born—in an integrated circuit of complementarity that ensures cosmic and telluric balance. Therefore, words, as breath and as pronunciation, not only act as ritual agents, but are also ritual, as language. Language rituals spatially and timelessly enact words, bringing together the past, the present, and the future, voice and rhythm, gesture and song, in a complementary way.

Ritual repetition provides the spark of speech as an event. To repeat is to recreate, to reiterate, to cause to happen. This reiteration, according to Muniz Sodré, signals "the uniqueness (therefore, the reality) of the moment experienced by the group. This moment is important. And it is vital for the community, because only it is capable of operating exchanges, of making the contacts that are essential to symbolic continuity."[48]

But the word is not isolated in its desire to be. Words underwrite a circumlocution of distinct sonorities that inscribe them in a polyphonic landscape, through which also circulates the vital force of movements. Sound bundles and word bundles. The vocalized and sung word, as breath, pronunciation, event, and rhythmic sound, is graphed and echoes in the performative reminiscence of the body, the site of events and wisdom. Words resonate as a singing and dancing voice, in a mutually significant expressive contiguous syntax that emanates all over the body. In this sound design, as Sodré teaches us, the sound "results from a process where a body is dynamically present, searching for contact with another body, to activate the àṣẹ."[49] Which also takes place in the cadence of the chants.

SPIRAL CHANTS AND CADENCES

An extensive and rich repertoire shelters the chants and all the musicality in Black cultures. In the performance of African and African diasporic oral textuality, wherever the subjects are, there is also the possibility of singing, of chants, of a chanted speech or a spoken-singing. Wherever the people are, there will be colloquies of sounds, voices, minimal elements, phrasings, pronunciations, syllabification, solfeggios, whistles, onomatopoeias, anaphoras, interjections, lines, timbres, rhythms, beats, percussions, call and responses, choruses, solos, countless vocalizations, syncopations, drums—that is, there will be components of a griot aesthetic. In Brazil and in other African-referenced territories in the Americas, from the farthest north to the farthest south, the musical constructions and inventions created at the crossroads manifest the Black-African musical heritage and collections, reaffirming the transit of African musical syntax as a determinant of Black rhythmic constructions, as in blues, jazz, and samba, for instance.

According to Jones, the "immediate predecessors of blues were the African American/American Negro work songs, which had their musical origins in West Africa."[50] Music has an aggregating social power and, according to Malone, "provides enjoyment and allows people to celebrate festivals and funerals; to compete with one another; to recite history, proverbs, and poetry; and to encounter gods. It teaches social patterns and values and helps people to work, to grow up, and to praise or criticize the behavior of community members."[51] In this rhythmic context, there is no Western distinction between vocal and instrumental music. For the peoples from the African diasporas, as well as peoples from Africa, "the human voice and musical instruments 'speak' the same language, express the same feelings, and unanimously recreate the universe each time that thought is transformed into sound."[52] A very high level of vocality prevails in musical construction itself, as if the instruments and the singing were often prioritized over spoken language. As noted by Jones, "just as the lyrics of the African songs were usually as important or *more* important than the music, the lyrics of the work songs and the later blues were equally important to the Negro's concept of music. In fact, the 'shouts' and 'field hollers' were little more than highly rhythmical lyrics."[53] Chants/songs, in their various modulations, are transmitters of energy, aesthetic idioms dispersed in Black oral textuality. They revitalize various genres, forms, and compositions of African repertoires in their rich and complex utterance, while also creating new tunes. In song and in speech we find *gestas*, stories, fables, tales, *vissungos*, proverbs, stories about divinities and families, the creation of the cosmos and beings, stories about crossings, work, and everyday life, the terrors of slavery, struggles and interdictions, but also the wars for freedom; teachings, animals, plants, technological practices, medicinal herbs, healing, devotion, sacredness, *inguiziras* and *quizumbas*, *ladainhas*, and *corridinhos*, prayers, challenges, outbursts, the act of making things and its techniques, mixtures of clay, the design and shape of houses, moonlight and sunlight, their risings and settings, streams, currents, delights, adornments, and aromas.[54]

In all of that and much more, chants/songs tell the history of Black peoples and, in performative textures, they embrace everything in their griot poetics, in which there are no monologues. "In the celebration of the collective pleasure of oral narration ... through the voice of the storyteller, the griot, the symbolic load of the autochthonous culture begins to circulate, allowing its maintenance and contribution so that this same culture can resist the impact of that other imposed over it by the white-European dominator, which finds in written text its strongest ally. The millenary art of orality spreads ancestral voices, seeking to maintain the law of this group, becoming thus an 'exercise in wisdom.'"[55] This same complexity is evident in melodic diversity, in voice emission techniques, and in unique alterations of tone and timbre employed by singers in their vocal interpretations, as well as in the performance of call and response chants. Call and response, rooted in African stylistic conventions, involves a sung conversation between a soloist who presents a theme and a group of voices, the chorus, responding to it. The soloist may extend the singing, at times improvising variations on the theme, or repeating it, exploring its enunciative possibilities. The repetition of and improvisation on the theme constitute the bonds of the spirals of ancestrality. The spiraling movement is also manifested in chants, as Glaura Lucas informs us in her insightful investigation on the complex musical texture found in Reinado chants:

> The musical constructions of Congado — chants/songs, *embaixadas*,[56] and rhythmic patterns — develop accordingly to a typical dynamic of the universe of oral traditions. Every year, the old reappears anew, transcreated in another time, and the new becomes old, (re)created from ancestral reference. . . . [57] Both in the rhythmic aspect of the instruments and in the melodic aspect of the singing, chants possess a cyclic character, determined by an intense repetition of patterns. . . . Starting from a basis, at a minimum setting, these patterns are subject to different degrees of variation over time. Rhythmic development thus proceeds in a spiral fashion.[58]

In the same context of Reinados, better known generally as Congados, it is worth noting that when the next singer "catches" a chant, before starting another theme or chant, they keep the spirals in a collective movement, repeating the previous chant three times. We can also think of the call and response technique as part of the fulfillment of this spiral dynamic. Chants go back and forth, undulating, curved, being themselves a knowledge of time as spiral sonorities.

Many forms of composition express this complex zone of textual production that alludes to Blackness as a plural and polyvalent epistemic system and to Africanity as a broad spectrum and as a territory with nuances, languages, and knowledge, and offer us a vast and rich repertoire for our reflection and delight. This myriad of compositions carries ethical values, as well as composition processes and techniques.

In Reinados' minimal sound cells, such as the "*ô ô ô*," "*olelê*," and "*tilelê*," in Oríkì-poems, or in more extensive chants—in their movements—singing connects this aesthetic, ethnic, and ethical heritage through ingenious ways of circumscribing and performing. Oríkìs, for example, encompass multiple ways of forming this complex and nodal performance, involving the designation of "names, epithets, poems," and covering "the spectrum of oral creation on a poetic level from one end to the other," as identified by Risério.[59]

In the Oríkì-poem, the author observes the expansion of a minimal thematic cell that unfolds and expands, "adding other units that are linked to it by ties of linguistic kinship, or by syntactic affinities"; "the hyperbolic turn of the word"; the "broad, coruscating, and blunt" images; the oddness of metaphors, the interlinked nomination "of a series of syntagms that, when arranged in a sequence or juxtaposed, actualize a paradigm of excess," configuring the physiognomy of the recreated object, the techniques of fitting, and the game of decentered intertextualities framed by the pulse of paratactic composition.[60]

It is also interesting to observe that the chants and proverbs play a significant educational role as theoretical, philosophical, and ethical contributions, serving "to teach, to explain and to thoroughly code and decode [*kânga ye kutula*]."[61] In African cultures, as well as in African Brazilian chants/songs, proverbs function as language systems, fulfilling exemplary pedagogical and ethical dimensions:

> The proverb is one among the most important sources that best explain the African Mûntu and his thought.... Proverbs, in African context, are laws, reflections, theories, customs, social norms and values, principles, and unwritten constitutions. They are used to justify what should be said or what has been said. Proverbs play a very important ethical role in storytelling, legends, etc. Very often parents as well as griots (*n'samuni*), and storytellers end their tales by very fitting proverbs. African proverbs are numerous and diverse. They deal with people, God, ancestors, animals, forests, goods, money, ideas, wars, sun, moon, time, social problems, education, food, life, *ku mpémba* (ancestors' world) traditions (*kinkulu*), history (*kikulu*), plants, insects, etc.[62]

These principles of codification, decodification, teachings, and criticism are very common in language games of oral practices and in chants; they are highlighted in warnings or challenges, as a song from Reinados says: "*Quem não pode com mandinga não carrega patuá*" (Those who can't handle the "sorcery," can't carry a "mojo bag").

Another relevant quality in the imbrication of speech, singing, and musicalization refers to the prevalence and primacy of vowel prolongation, which instills a sound reverberation of its own in the Brazilian version of the Portuguese language. This high level of vocality finds one of its sources in African languages, particularly in the Bantu languages, whose importance and formative extension were decisive in the reshaping of Portuguese in Brazil, due to their impact on the formation of the lexicon and vocabulary, and due to their phonetic texture, in the musicality and melody of pronunciation, where the vowels are prolonged as if sung. There are several incidences of Bantu languages in Brazilian Portuguese.[63] In addition to reshaping the lexicon, they were employed as secret languages, systems, and codes for communicating specific messages, whether from everyday life, or from flight plans, or even within the realm of religious practices and systems, in which they were and still are employed to shelter principles which must not be revealed, which must be protected. As in its designation as *Língua de Nego* (Negro language), in the realm of Reinado, or as *Língua de Angola* (Angola language), in the Angola Nation Candomblés, for instance. These are also codes of dual speech, an alternate way of communicating, circumventing prohibitions, erasing the system.[64] Some of them are still used nowadays in chants and even in communication between community members. They are signs of prestige for those who master them.

Percussion can also be heard as an extension of the voice. Jones maintains that, even in the strictly instrumental realm, there is a certain predominance of vocality over other elements, because "even the purely instrumental music of the American Negro contains constant reference to vocal music. Blues-playing is the closest imitation of the human voice of any music I've heard; the vocal effects that jazz musicians have delighted in."[65] The sound-musical ambience, as a synthesis, is a metonymy of the entire structure of Black ancestral thought, a cartography, a marker of consonance and movement. The spoken word, vocalities and sonorities, all musical textures and particularities, timbres and rhythms, movements and gestures, as well as the polychromatic and luminous designs, are conceived as an indivisible unit, mutually complementary. Singing invites dancing, which, in turn, embroiders musical sculptures in the air. This musical tapestry can be read as a cosmogram, since it retains, in its spiral radiances and frequencies, the very same qualities as these wisdom cartographies. That is, sound rhythms, in themselves, as mise en abyme, reverberate culture in its integrity and the time that structures them.

FIGURE 3.2. *Something to Do with a Mission* (play, Cia Os Crespos, 2016). *From left to right:* Dani Nega, Sidney Santiago Kuanza, Niara Ngozi, Lucélia Sérgio, Giovanni Di Ganzá, Joyce Barbosa, and William Simplício. Photo: Roniel Felipe.

A BODY OF ADORNMENTS, LUMINOSITIES, AND POLYCHROMY

Clothing and the way of dressing are integral to bodily practices, adding both value and dynamics to movements and silhouettes. These elements, in turn, produce images, sculpting movements, gestures, and postures. They also draw scenographies, spatialities, and luminosities, ultimately translating concepts and habits.

Clothing composition transmits messages. It has the power to either expand or inhibit movements, subordinate or expand the limits of physical actions. Clothing can make movements and positions more flexible or restrictive, facilitating or restraining steps and dances. Additionally, it provides dynamism or moderation of rhythms when combined with musicalities. Furthermore, clothing can also impose behaviors, provide shelter, or censor delights. Much like facial features, clothing shapes and sculpts the body.[66]

Bodily movements, facial expressions, modes of speaking, singing, and clothing are stylistic formulations, and they refer to languages and cultural styles. As

Maultsby states, "Performers establish an image, communicate a philosophy, and create an atmosphere of 'aliveness' through the colorful and flamboyant costumes they wear."[67] Along with Maultsby's perspective, Connerton observes that the way of dressing configures a grammar as important as the syntax of writing: "To read or wear clothes is in a significant respect similar to reading or composing a literary text.... Just as one group has internalised the grammar of literature which enables them to convert linguistic sentences into literary structures and meanings, so likewise has the other internalised the grammar of dress which enables them to convert clothing items into clothing structures and meanings."[68] Suzana Martins, referring to the "aesthetic icons" mentioned by Thompson, rightly highlights the significant character of clothing and attires in Yoruba traditions:

> One of these icons refers to the exuberant use of colors that harmonize the luminosity of warm, bright, and vivid colors with the softness of discreet colors, thus creating a chromatic contrast that evokes an intense and beautiful look. Another icon refers to the patterns of drawn lines and the texture of the fabrics, which allows for the application, in the same composition, of simple and sophisticated designs, such as the combination of geometric lines and shapes (squares, curves, parallel lines, etc.) and the use of various types of fabrics (chintz, brocade, lace, including *richelieu* embroidery, etc.).[69]

This aesthetic of adornments does not simply indicate an emphasis on illustration or decorative embellishment. The clothes and attires, hair designs, inscriptions and adornments, the use of various accessories, chromatic arrangements, and the play of polychromy and luminosities that make up body prints compose aesthetic codes with strong intensity and cultural symbolism.

It should be noted that, in Africa, as well as in African American (in a broader sense) cultures, one of the ways the body writes is through the use of shells, seeds, and other hollow objects of different sizes and colors in the manufacture of necklaces, bracelets, earrings, and other arabesques, in order to adorn skin and hair. Arranged in a certain position and contiguous order, Job's tears, seeds, shells, and body painting function as morphemes that form words, words that form sentences, and sentences composing narratives, literally making the body surface a text while making the subject simultaneously an interpreter and interpretant, utterance, concept and form.

These processes bring forth techniques for manufacturing recycled materials, and also a meaning and a semiosis that attest to their power to produce significance. Accessories are part of the contiguous movement of creating principles, meanings, and modes of carrying them out, as Mestre Didi teaches us: "The manufacture of a necklace with a ritualistic purpose among the Yoruba needs a certain knowledge, the exact combination of beads, size, number of turns, and shape are of great importance for [the object's] meaning."[70]

The entire history of the constitution of Black cultures in general seems to reveal the primacy of these processes of displacement, substitution, and resemantization, suturing the gaps and holes caused by all the losses. The implementation of this alternate knowledge, which still fertilizes several Black communities today, modulates the strategies of cultural and social resistance that drove enslaved people's revolts, the effective action of *quilombolas*,[71] and many other Black organizations against the slave system.

The body of adornments is an extension of the canvas-body, an image-body that is skin, background, and volume, a body of *inputs* and *outputs* digitizing its environment and its spatialities. It is impregnated with multiple meanings, possibilities for the composition of the event, and an exquisite semiotic production. A hieroglyphic body. A body that is also memory and translates the same artistic attributes that drive Mnemosyne, the mater of the poetic function: tradition and improvisation, memory and oblivion, continuity and fleetingness, permanence and ephemerality, incompleteness and completeness, presence and absence, being and becoming.

The aesthetic of adornments points to the writings on the body, as well as to the cultural corpus that signifies them. The canvas-body is also a polychromatic fabric, illuminated by warm and cold colors, vibrant tones interspersed or superimposed on soft nuances, in a grammar of unique combinations, at times composed of shade and drawing pattern discontinuities and asymmetries, at times geometrically conceived and arranged. Here are included the specificity of white clothes and fabrics as the basis of spirituality, as well as the multicolored tapestry; the different models of skirts, petticoats, underskirts; turbans of multiple styles; earrings, bracelets, rosaries and prayer beads; necklaces; instruments tied to legs and arms; as well as the decoration of the surroundings, the decoration of chapels, poles, flags, trees, altars, niches, with a boundless variety of palettes, bright and vibrant stellar installations, composing the designs of a dazzling and sui generis luminosity aesthetic.

A body that sews and emanates aromas. The subjects and the artistic forms that emerge from it are "made of memory, making history."[72]

ALCHEMY OF FLAVORS AND AROMAS

In ritual performance, the canvas-body enraptures, and from it emanate all the elements that compose and are imbued in it: the choreographic movements, sound waves, vocality, vibratos, rhythms and cadences, timbres, seals and signets; the composition of the air in the spinning silhouettes and figures that act like lightning; and also the smells, aromas, and the sacred chemistry of herbs and spices.

In this *kizomba*,[73] the intimate relationship with the environment translates the human connection with other beings of existence and with the cosmos, in what can be seen and beheld, in the presence of the stars sparkling in the skies, as well as in what cannot be seen—which can only be glimpsed or remains concealed—but which sharpens our senses for its perception, without ever being less heard or sensed, in its immanence of presence. Ancestors, in themselves, are an accumulation of nature.

Education with nature finds its roots in the thought that everything is connected to nature, that everything in it (is) ex/changes, for food and medicine, healing scents, incense, perfumes, lights, and all flavors come from nature. The relationship with nature is thus also an ethical stance. Hence the care with ecology, which means reverence to nature and desire for balance. It is not surprising, therefore, that Black *terreiros* are inhabited by trees of various species, bushes, tall plants, small plants, gardens, flowerbeds, et cetera.

The sacred dwells in nature. In the Candomblés, some trees mirror and are constitutive of the deities and entities of ancestrality. In the Bantu traditions as well, what is sacred is settled in the backyards, in a rich flora: in trunks, roots, branches, leaves, and flowers. The poles in Reinados, for instance, must be made of wood, because, like the trees, they are also a kind of transmitter and an interconnection between ground-earth-humanity and the forces of the high cosmos. The body thus, in these traditions, is a ground-body and simultaneously a pole-body.

What is taken from nature must be respected and replaced, in a relationship of equivalence, a mutual exchange of substances, power, and materials that guarantees not only subsistence, but the utmost possibility of cosmic existence. According to Oliveira, "Nature is the source of life. The relationship between the sacred and nature is symbiotic. As an old African proverb says: '*Kosi ewé, kosi orisá*,' that is 'without herbs (nature) there is no Orisha (deities).' Nature and divinity are, in fact, oftentimes, the sign of one and the same."[74]

Cunha also reminds us that "there can be no Candomblés and Umbandas (designating the various religions of African origin) without leaves, there can be no Candomblés and Umbandas without norms of respect for nature and its forces or energies."[75] The same relationship is fundamental in Reinados and in all cultural manifestations of Bantu descent, since, for them, nature is, then and thus, as Fu-Kiau states, a "laboratory without walls":

> The Bântu, Kôngo and Luba peoples accept the natural world as sacred in its totality because through it, they see the greatness of Kalunga. The superior energy of life, Kalunga is entirely complete (*lunga*) in itself. Thus, when a Mûntu (human being) sees a tiny crystal (*ngêngele*), they see in it not merely its sacredness but also the divine presence of *Kalûnga*.
>
> In addition to the attention and admiration given to mountains, valleys, the wind, the sky, and the changes in the natural cycle, the Mûntu pays special attention to the world of the forest because, as it is said, *Mfinda Kasuka tufukidi*—we perish if the forests are extinct. Due to this popular view among the Bântu, the very act of entering the forest becomes a sacred ritual.[76]

The canvas-body is a gourd bowl with flavors, spices, smells, and aromas. The culinary arts, the alchemy between elements of nature, bake and make up this canvas-body.

In the backyards of houses and *terreiros*, the body integrates itself into a green landscape, painted by the multiple colors and properties of food, leaves, herbs, and roots, whether in their natural state or cooked and spiced. The smells and odors of incense and the essences of plants, fruits, and flowers, cleanse and restore the body, predisposing the person to the ritual. As channels of reverberation, they impregnate the spaces and environments as gateways of vital force irradiation.

Cooking, preparing, and performing mean maintaining relationships and sacred bonds with nature. Thus, the person cooking transmits, in the act of cooking, a skill and a substance that nourishes, but also transmits their inner quality, their feelings and apprehensions, their good or bad energy, the "food tastes good only if one can taste and feel the mind and heart of the person who cooked it. This applies to cultures as well," because "we are what we consume, learn, hear, see and feel. . . . We feel waves/vibrations and radiation [*minika ye minienie*] because we ourselves produce waves/vibrations and radiation. We are sensitive to heat, cold, and electricity [*tiya, kiôzi ye ngolo za n'cezi/sula*] only because we ourselves as organisms produce heat, cold, and electricity."[77] This thought translates a chemical, organic, but also ethical relationship. An asset. A value. A property and a seal of the African-referenced arts, found in their philosophies, worldview, and in the various ways this experience radiates.

COMPOSITION IV

MY DESTINY IS TO SING, THE MYTHOPOETIC *GESTA* OF THE REINADOS

Entre silêncio e som
Riem tambores e sombras.
Os meninos criaram memória
Ántes de criar cabelos.

[Between silence and sound
drums and shadows laugh.
Children created memory
before they even grew hair.]
— EDIMILSON DE ALMEIDA PEREIRA, "Curiangu"

Ô tindô le lê
Ô tindô la lá
Deixa a caixa batê
Deixa o povo pulá

[O tindo le le
O tindo la la
Let the drums beat
Let the people bounce]
— REINADO CHANT

FIGURE 4.1. Group of Congo Players. Reinado de Nossa Senhora do Rosário do Jatobá, 2017. Photo: Vera Godoy. Archive of the author.

ON *GESTAS* AND NARRATIVES

In performances of the voice, chants and narratives recreate history from a Black perspective in all cultural derivations of African origin that were restored in Brazil and throughout the Americas, in countless oral repertoires—spoken and sung—by the masters of voice and rites and their griot vocalities. In these tales and narrative songs, multiple knowledges unfold before our ears—a remarkable feat that encompasses the historical crossings of Black folks. These stories delve into their memories of Africa, recount African and African Brazilian tales, explore the formation of the cosmos, narrate deities' stories, share anecdotes and accounts, and present many other utterances—both ancient and contemporary. These performances of *oralitura* rejuvenate these narratives in the sacred space of all Black *terreiros*—cosmic realms where knowledges are settled, created, and disseminated. The ingenious construction mode of diverse and polyphonic oral textuality in these performances often involves the exercise of secret codes—knowledges censored by slavery, skillfully passed on through generations. As I stated in *A cena em sombras* (The scene in shadows), Black culture in the Americas is dual-sided, dual-voiced. It expresses, in its foundational ways, the distinction between what the social system assumed that subjects should say and do, and what, through numerous practices, they actually said and did. In this operation of asymmetric balance and displacement, metamorphosis and layering are some of the fundamental principles and tactics—essential operators of African American (in a broader sense) cultural formation—that the study of performative traditions and practices reiterates and reveals. In the Americas, African arts, crafts, and knowledges take on new and ingenious formats. As stated by Wole Soyinka, under adverse conditions, cultural forms transform to ensure their survival.[1] Or, as Roach argues: "In the life of a community, the process of surrogation does not begin or end but continues as actual or perceived vacancies occur in the network of relations that constitutes the social fabric. Into the cavities created by loss through death or other forms of departure, I hypothesize, survivors attempt to fit satisfactory alternates."[2] In the realm of the crossroads—which are foundations for reinscribing these knowledges in the Americas—ingenious ways of constructing narratives interweave ancient histories and textual repertoires in their various modes of assertion, in the twists of languages, rituals, and many other performing practices that enact them. In this environment of reminiscences, the Black Reinados, for example, already revisited by me in the book *Afrografias da memória* (Afrographies of memory), restore a plethora of mnemonic procedures and stylistic techniques. Through these techniques, some of the most precious African philosophical principles are reprocessed and inscribed into the Brazilian ethnocultural fabric as markers of civilization. Among these principles, the notions of ancestrality and spiral time take center stage.

UNDAMBA MANGANÁ

The Reinados are an alternate religious system and a form of Black organization established at the very crossroads between Christian religious systems and African religious systems of Bantu descent, through which devotion to certain Catholic saints, such as Nossa Senhora do Rosário (Our Lady of the Rosary), São Benedito (Saint Benedict), Santa Ifigênia (Saint Iphigenia), and Nossa Senhora das Mercês (Our Lady of Mercy), among others, are carried out through African-style ritual performances, in their metaphysical symbolism, conventions, choreography, structure, values, aesthetic conceptions, and in the very cosmoperception that establishes them. Performed through a complex symbolic and liturgical structure, the rites include the participation of distinct groups, called *guardas*,[3] and the establishment of an *Império Negro* (Black Empire); in this context, plays and dramatic dances, the coronation of kings and queens, *embaixadas* (embassies), and liturgical, ceremonial, and performing acts, create a mythopoetic performance that reinterprets the crossings of Black folks from Africa to the Americas. Travelers' accounts and other oral and written accounts trace the Reinados' existence back to the seventeenth century in Recife, and it has spread to other regions of the Brazilian territory, in many cases linked to the *Irmandades dos Pretos* (Black Fraternities).

The festivities of the Reinados are rites of distress and reconnection founded by a cosmogonic plot that develops through an elaborated symbolic structure, whose festive performance brings us back to the setting of the ritual, described by Victor Turner as an orchestration of actions, symbolic objects, and sensory, visual, auditory, kinesthetic, olfactory, and gustatory codes, full of music and dance.[4] As such, they carry aesthetic and cognitive values, transcreated by means of strategies of concealment and visibility, procedures and techniques of expression which, kinesthetically and dynamically, modify, expand, and recreate the cultural codes intertwined in the performance and in the realm of rite, whose context (i.e., quotidian reality), however oppressive, is symbolically, socially, and historically replaced and altered.

All ritual acts emerge from a narrative of origin, which narrates the removal of an image of Nossa Senhora do Rosário from the waters. One of the versions tells us that, at the time of slavery, an image of Nossa Senhora do Rosário appeared at sea. Black folks saw the saint in the waters, with a crown whose brightness outshone the sun. They called the master of the farm and asked him to let them remove the Senhora from the water. The landowner did not allow it, but ordered them to build a little church and properly decorate it for her. After the chapel was built, the *sinhô* (master) gathered his white peers, removed the image from the water, and placed it on an altar. The next day, the chapel was empty, and the saint was floating in the water again. After several unsuccessful attempts to keep the deity in the chapel, the white man allowed Black folks to try to rescue her. The first ones to go to the sea were a group of Congos. They adorned themselves with flamboyant colors and, with their quick dances, tried to captivate the saint. She enjoyed their songs and dances and rose from the waters, but did not follow them. The older ones, already very feeble, went to the forest, chopped wood, made three drums out of the tree trunks—the sacred *candombe* drums—and covered them with yam leaves. They gathered the group and entered the waters while singing and dancing. With their syncopated, booming rhythm, telluric dance, and songs of strong African timbres, they captivated the saint, who sat on one of their drums and accompanied them to the chapel, where everyone, Black and white, sang and danced to celebrate her.[5]

This story, told and sung in several tones, is recreated as the following by Mrs. Alzira Germana Martins, one of the noblest voices of Reinado:

In the old days, my late mother, may God rest her soul, told us stories of saints. She used to tell a legend that actually happened at the time of the slaves. A long time ago, Our Lady of the Rosary appeared to the slaves, it was at the time of slavery. A slave ordered his son to go get some water near the sea. When the boy got there, he saw a very strong light in the sea. He looked and looked, then stopped to see it better. He felt it was a girl holding a child in the sea. He ran back, called his father, and said in their tongue that there was a lady in the sea, drowning with a child in her arms. The father didn't believe the boy and went to see it with his own eyes. When he got there, he also saw the lady at sea, her crown shone too bright, like a very strong light. Then that slave went to the farm and told Massa what he saw. Massa didn't believe him and ordered him to be whipped. The man said: you can beat me, Massa, you can whip me, but the virgin is drowning in the sea. Massa then got white people together on a pilgrimage only to take the saint out of the sea. When they arrived there and saw the saint drowning, they began praying and singing aloud to the saint. The white man got her out of the sea and took her to the farm, he also made an altar and put her there. After praying, they went to sleep. The other day, he looked for the saint, but she wasn't there. He thought the slaves had stolen the saint and ordered the slaves to be beaten. When the slaves cried and said it wasn't them, the white man returned to the sea and saw that the saint was almost drowning already. He took her to the altar again, but she escaped again. When he understood she didn't want to accept them, he let them slaves try.

Them slaves came together and made drums, covered them with yam leaves. They took the wood, cut it round, and braided banana tree fiber around it. They went into the swamp and got yam leaves to cover the drums. First went the well-adorned *guarda* of Congo. They danced for her, but she didn't come out of the water. She thought it was very beautiful, but she didn't come out. Then them older slaves gathered all them slaves, old and young, they prepared a *guarda* of Moçambique and danced for her. It was the same folks, it was the same drums, but the singing and dancing was different. When they danced for her, in the different way the Moçambique dance, she stared a lot at them. They were going into the sea, singing to her, taking the baton near her. They sang like this:

Oh, Mary comes
with God already,
Mary comes

They were coming and coming with the baton near her, like this, and she held the baton; when she did so, they sang to her:

Oh, Mary comes
with God already,
Mary comes

As she held that baton, they managed to pull her out of the sea, then covered one of the drums with the white cloth they carried on their shoulders and she sat on top of that drum, on top of the drum sits Our Lady of the Rosary. And she became the patroness of the whole black race, our Missus, our mother. The water went and came and they came and went. That is why the Moçambique are the owners of the crown, because they took Our Lady from the sea and sat her on their drums. And they carried her very slowly, singing:

Olê, slow we go
Olê, slow we go
Moçambique can't run
Moçambique can't run
Olê, slow we go[6]

During the festivities, this founding myth is recreated and alluded to in processions, speeches, songs, dances, and fabulations, in a multifaceted plot in which mystical and mythical elements interact with other themes and narratives that recreate the history of crossings of Black Africans and their Brazilian descendants. Depending on the region and communities, the protagonists of the event may be many. Its ritual festivities feature a complex structure, including *novenas*, raising poles, processions, dramatic dances, feasts, *embaixadas*, fulfillment of vows,[7] under the baton of kings, queens, captains, masters, and the wise of the Reinados.

In the state of Minas Gerais, the diversity of *guardas* includes, among others, Congos, Moçambiques, Marujos, Marujadas, Catopés, Vilões, Caboclos, and Caboclinhos. Amid these, two groups stand out: Congo and Moçambique, the ones that handled the removal of the saint from the waters. The group of Congos represents the vanguard, those who start the processions and clear the paths, overcoming obstacles with their swords and/or long colorful batons. The members of the *terno de Moçambique*, which is closer to the original sound of the Candombes, usually wear blue, white, or pink skirts over all-white clothing; they wear turbans on their heads and *gungas* (rattles) on their ankles; they carry big bass drums. They dance in groups, without any planned choreography. Their movement is slow, and their drums echo a vibrant and syncopated rhythm. The feet of the *Moçambiqueiros* (members of the Moçambique group) never move far from the earth, and their dance, which vibrates throughout their bodies, is sharply expressed through their half-curved shoulders, torsos, and feet. The *terno* or *guarda de Moçambique* guards the *majestades* (majesties), which represent the greater spiritual power and telluric force of the ancestors, which emanate from the sacred drums and guide the community rite. Through lyrical and rhythmic enunciation, their chants accentuate both the slow pulsation of their movements and the sacred mysteries.

All the different variations of this legend, from all Brazilian regions, allow an emphasis on the shared narrative, through which the reengineering of knowledges and powers found in the structure of the Black Reinados is processed. In the performances, there are basically three elements that persist on the network of utterances and the construction of the narrative: (1) the description of a situation of repression experienced by the enslaved Black person; (2) the symbolic reversal of this situation with the removal of the saint from the waters, with the singing and dancing being ruled by the drums; (3) the implementation of a hierarchy and of another power: an African one, founded by this mythical and mystical framework.

By removing the saint from the waters and rendering movement to her, the Black individual performs an act of appropriation and reshaping, shifting, through sacred pronunciation, the power positions between white and Black people. The language of the drums, the ancestors' breath, invested in a divine *ethos*, operates the chants and dances and, in an oracular manner, foreshadows a subversion of the social order, of slaving hierarchies and hegemonic knowledges. This displacement interferes with the syntax of the Catholic text, which is now inseminated by an alternate language that, as a style and a (cutting) stylus, is graphed and now beats in the conjugation of the sound of drums, chants, and dances, intertwined in an articulation of speech and voice with African timbres. The very foundation of the mythical Catholic text is crossed out, and African deities are injected into it, as in a palimpsest. Thus, Our Lady of the Rosary also evokes, by displacement, the great African chthonic mothers, ladies of the water, earth, and air.

In a perspective that transcends the symbolic-religious context, this act of displacement and repossession induces the possibility of reversibility and transformation of power relations within this adverse social-historical context. It is increasingly significant that narratives and performances highlight the coming together of different African peoples and ethnicities, overlapping with historical ethnic and linguistic differences and antagonisms. Thus, collectivity overlaps the individual, as an operator of forms of social and cultural resistance that reactivate, restore, and reterritorialize, through emblematic metamorphoses, an alternate knowledge, embodied in the memory of the body and the voice. Both in the utterance of the mythical narration and in the performance that kinesthetically re-presents it, the partial overcoming of ethnic diversities recreates the common *ethos* and (the) Black collective act(ion) as strategies for replacing and reorganizing the fractures of knowledge. Between the lines of fabular utterance, it is possible to read a pendulous gesture: One sings for the divinity and to celebrate Black majesties—*majestades*—and, simultaneously, sings and dances against the seizure of freedom and against oppression, in the past—as in slavery—or in the present.

From this gesture emerges the second movement dramatized in the narratives: the establishment of an alternate power structure that reorganizes Black ethnic relations, as well as the strategic positions imbricated therein. The *majestades*, who embody power and authority, are—as in distant and imaginary Africa—the mediators between the human and the divine. Sacredness radiates from them; and, through them, the vital force is activated. This force emanates throughout the complex ritual fabric, covering the whole community with blessings. The *majestades* are guides, masters, subjects of healing, prayers, and blessings who illuminate the sacred that dwells in everything and that is also manifested and spread by voice. To them, we sing:

Ora viva Rainha de Congo
viva
ora viva Rainha de Congo
viva
a Rainha que veio do terreiro d'Angola
viva
a Rainha da tribo dona d'ingomá
viva
Ô viva viva viva
Rainha de Congo viva

[Long live the Queen of Congo
she lives
Long live the Queen of Congo
she lives
the Queen who came from the terreiro d'Angola
she lives
the Queen of the dona d'ingomá tribe
she lives
Oh long live long live long live
the Queen of Congo lives]

The *guardas* of Congo open the processions and clear the paths, as a vanguard warrior force. The Moçambique, chosen as leader of the sacred rites and guardian of the crowns that represent the African peoples and the Lady of the Rosary, leads kings and queens. The timbre of their drums represents, in a speculative relationship engendered by fabulation, the most genuinely African voice, reminiscent of the origin that iconically translates the memory of Africa. Lord of the crowns and guardian of mysteries, the Moçambique is the telluric warrior force that manages the African continuum, symbolically reorganizing the asymmetric power relations between Black peoples and the colonizer, as well as among numerous ethnicities. Therefore, new founding hierarchies of the social microsystem are established in the parallel structure of spatial relations of the Black Reinados. These hierarchies operationalize communication networks and power relations between Black folks themselves and between Black folks and white folks.

This account also reveals a process of substitution in the production of liturgical objects and accessories, as well as the resignification of the geographical and symbolic environment. Therefore, enslaved Black people make their sacred drums out of trunks, leaves, and vines, and use Job's tears and other materials available in the American geographies instead of *Opeles* and other accessories. As I have already mentioned, it should be noted that in Africa, as well as in the African American (in a broader sense) cultures, one of the ways the body writes is through the use of shells, seeds, and other hollow objects of different sizes and colors in the manufacture of necklaces, bracelets, and other adornments that cover the subjects, in addition to other arabesques that adorn their skin and hair. Arranged in a certain contiguous position and order, the beads, seeds, and shells, as well as certain drawings, function as morphemes that form words, words that form sentences, and sentences that form texts, literally making the body's surface a text, and the subject simultaneously a sign, an interpreter and interpretant, utterance, concept, and form. This ingenious process constitutes what I have named an *aesthetic of adornments.*[8] Written in and through adornments, "the person emerges from such readings, made of memory, and making memory."[9]

The whole history of the Reinados (violently repressed and persecuted from the second half of the nineteenth century to the middle of the twentieth century), and of Black cultures in general, seems to reveal the primacy of these processes of displacement, substitution, and resemantization, suturing the gaps and holes caused by all the losses. The implementation of this alternate power, which still fertilizes several Black communities today, prefigures the strategies of cultural and social resistance that drove enslaved people's revolts, the effective action of *quilombolas* (maroons), and many other Black organizations against the slave system. As the popular aphorism goes, "the beads of my rosary are artillery shells." Or as Roach puts it, "texts may obscure what performance tends to reveal: memory challenges history in the construction of circum-Atlantic cultures, and it revises the yet unwritten epic of their fabulous cocreation."[10]

In the mythopoetic narrative—chants, gestures, dances, and in all the liturgical derivations of the Reinado ceremony—the *congadeiro* sings and dances the Catholic deity, affectionately called Undamba Berê Berê or Undamba Manganá in Kimbundu, lady of the earth, of the waters, of heaven and air, and with her the Nanas of African waters, Nzambi, the supreme Bantu god, the ancestors and all the sophisticated African gnosis, a result of a telluric philosophy that recognizes in nature a certain measure of the human, not in an animistic manner, but as an expression of a necessary cosmic complementarity, which does not separate the divine breath and the matter, in all forms and elements of the cosmic physis.[11]

The poetic narrative, therefore, shapes the rite of passage from a situation of distress, fragmentation, and disorder into a new social, political, artistic, and philosophical order that reshapes the cultural corpus, subverts the dominator/dominated relationship, and impregnates the Catholic religious fabric with African telluric theology and the thoughts that arise from it.[12]

All the memory of this knowledge is established in and by the ritual performance of the Reinados, through techniques and performative procedures conveyed by the body, in several of its attributes, such as the voice, in a refined and complex aesthetical and handcrafted stylization. The universe of cognition expressed in all ceremonies and liturgies transcreates, in the Americas, African artistic styles, modes of living, and modes of belonging, a distinct perception and comprehension of the cosmos, as well as a singular reflection on the sacred that transcends Western metaphysical languages.

IN THE BODY, TIME DANCES

In the complex zones of sound-making nuanced by Blackness, the vocalized word resonates as an effect of an instinctive body language, inscribing the emitter/subject in a specific circuit of expression, potency, and power.[13] As breath, pronunciation, and event, the spoken word is graphed in the performance of the body, which is the place of wisdom. Therefore, words, markers of knowledge, are not calcified in a motionless deposit or archive, but rather are kinesthetically designed. As such, words echo in the performative reminiscence of the body, resonating as a singing and dancing voice, in a contiguous expressive syntax fertilizing the kinship between the living, the ancestors, and those yet to be born. A dynamic force and principle, words become language "because they express and externalize a process of synthesis in which all the elements that constitute the subject intervene."[14] That is why language needs music, dance, rhythm, colors, the performative gesture, and adequate conditions for its realization. Hence, the numinous nature of the voice and the auratic power of the body in African Brazilian religions, both resonances of these religions' Africanness, in which the creation, the record, and the emanation of knowledge are also manifested and conveyed through the spoken and sung word, through music, and through an entire rhythmic sonority, choreographed through dance and in every movement and gesture. Sound itself sculpts its visualizations in the air.

As utterance, sonorities create sculptures of the voice, carving out the utterance of the subject and their collectivity. In their value as *graphya* and redaction, language erasure, and significant alteration, they constitute the alterity of subjects, cultures, and their symbolic representations, like a kinesthetic trace, a craft knife carving out knowledges, values, concepts, worldviews, and styles, supported by the ethics of the knowledges which ground them. A *graphya*, a language, designed in the performative undulations of sonorities and in the body's turns.

As stated by philosopher Bunseki Fu-Kiau, Africa is the "dancing continent," for music and dance permeate every activity, being a form of inscription and transmission of knowledges and values. In Africa, every sound and every gesture signifies, which leads Robert Farris Thompson to state that "Africa thus introduces a different art history, a history of a *danced* art."[15] In this danced aesthetic— that is, in this aesthetic in which movement is the prevalent structure—embodied practices are constitutive and constituent of the modes of making, turning the body and its poetics into agents of inscription of knowledge. According to Muniz Sodré, "With words and sound, there must be the concrete presence of a human body capable of speaking and listening, giving and receiving, in an ever reversible movement."[16] Thus, "to sing/dance, to follow the rhythm, is akin to listening to the beats of one's own heart—it is feeling life while symbolically remembering death," while rhythm itself is the movement "of the impulse that leads the body to search for its lack."[17]

The body in performance restores, expresses, and simultaneously produces this knowledge graphed in the memory of the gesture. Performing, in this sense, means inscribing, repeating by transcreating and revising, and it represents "an alternative and potentially contestatory form of knowledge."[18] The memory of knowledges is spread by countless acts of performance, beyond the record engraved with alphabet letters; through bodily performance—movements, gestures, dances, mime, dramatizations, celebration ceremonies, rituals, et cetera—the selective memory of prior knowledge is implemented and maintained in the social and cultural realms. Thus, in the realm of *oralituras*, the body is a portal that simultaneously inscribes and interprets, signifies and is signified, being projected as both continent and content, place, environment, and vehicle of memory, a "'place of meeting and transfer' . . . a mirror that limns the observer's gaze and the object of that gaze, reflecting one back upon the other."[19]

In the realm of the Reinados' performances and Black cultural manifestations, in their apparatus—chants/songs, dances, costumes, accessories, ceremonial objects, scenarios, processions, and celebrations—and in their philosophical and religious cosmoperception, the textual, historical, sensory, organic, and conceptual repertoires of distant Africa, are reorganized, as well as the scores of African knowledge and wisdom, the alternate body of re-created identities, memories, and reminiscences; in short, the corpus of memory that carves out and crosses the voids and gaps resulting from the diasporas. Thereby, rites fulfill an exemplary paradigmatic pedagogical function, as a model and marker of change and displacement; for, according to Turner, "as a 'model *for*,' ritual can anticipate, even generate change; as a 'model *of*,' it may inscribe order in the minds, hearts, and wills of participants."[20]

As I pointed out earlier, this process of intervention in the environment and this potential for formal and conceptual reconfiguration make rituals an effective way of transmission and reterritorialization of a complex plethora of knowledges. This includes a thought-provoking conception of temporalities: the spiral time, linked to the structuring conception of ancestrality, a cosmic conception that includes, in the same phenomenological circuit, the deities, cosmic nature, fauna, flora, physical elements, the dead, the living, and those who are yet to be born, all conceived as bonds of a necessary complementarity, in a continuous process of transformation and becoming.

This cosmic and philosophical perception interweaves time, ancestrality, and death in the same circuit of significance. The primacy of ancestral movement, a source of inspiration, nuances the curves of a spiral temporality, in which times, unveiled from a linear chronology, are in the process of perennial transformation. Birth, maturity, and death become, therefore, necessary natural contingencies in the mutational and regenerative dynamics of all vital and existential cycles. In the spirals of time, everything goes and comes back. For Fu-Kiau, in Kikongo societies, experiencing time means inhabiting a curvilinear temporality, conceived as a scroll that simultaneously conceals and reveals, rolls and unrolls the temporal instances that constitute the person.[21] The Kikongo aphorism "*Ma'kwenda! Ma'kwisa!*—'what goes on (now) will come back (later),'" translates, with wit and grit, the idea that "what flows in a cyclical motion will remain in the motion." This same idea is graphed in one of the most important kinds of African inscriptions, transcreated in various ways in the African Brazilian religions: the cosmograms, symbols of the cosmos and the continuity of existence, also present in the choreographies of the Reinados and in various manifestations of Black cultures in Brazil and the Americas.

The ancestors' mediation, also manifested in the Congados by the vital force of the *candombes* (sacred drums), is the master key of rites; from this mediation comes the power of the spoken word and the bodily gesture—instruments of inscription and retransmission of the ancestral legacy. This pendulous process between tradition and its transmission implements a curvilinear, reactivating, and prospective movement that synchronously integrates the present of the past and of the future in the present of the performed event. As a logos in motion, from the ancestor to the performer and from the performer to the ancestor and to the *infans*, each ritual performance recreates, restores, and revises a phenomenological circle in which pulsates, in the same contemporaneity, an action from a continuous past, an action synchronized in a present temporality that attracts the past and the future and spreads itself on them. By doing so, it does not abolish time, but its linear and consecutive conception. Thus, the idea of temporal successiveness is obliterated by the reactivation and actualization of the similar and diverse action, already performed both before and after the moment that restores it as event. In this synchrony, the past can be defined as the place of accumulative knowledge and experience that underwrites both the present and the future, being also underwritten by them.

For the *congadeiro*, this knowledge also implements itself spatially. A visited space is a consecrated, reterritorialized site. The processions and walks revisit recognized places, retracing circles around poles, crosses, and churches. They follow paths previously carved by their ancestors while treading new roads.

The undulating sonorities and the movements that engender or are stimulated by them build the choreographies of a spiral circularity, whether through the body's dancing or through the spatial occupation that this spinning body draws around itself. Through this constitutive evocation, the gesture and voice of ancestrality embody the present event, prefiguring becoming, in a curvilinear genealogical conception articulated by performance. Here, the movement of the voice-body, the ground-body, the pole-body occupies the space in unfolded circles, figuring the excentric and spiraling notion of simultaneous temporalities. In other words: Time, in its spiral dynamics, can only be conceived through space or in the spatiality of the gap occupied by the moving body. Time and space thus become mutually mirrored images.

It is told that, a long time ago, the enslaved African folks in the Americas drew cosmograms of their cultures of origin on the shells of sea turtles and on the plumage of certain birds in order to communicate to their ancestors, who rested in Africa, their whereabouts in the distant American landscapes. With the poetic forms that sustain us, in response to the gestures of ancestrality, we can echo Angolan poet Ruy Duarte:

Não há lugar achado
sem lugar perdido.
Casam-se além as falas de um lugar,
no encontro da memória
com a matriz.[22]

[There is no place found
without a place lost
The tongues of a place unite beyond
in the meeting of memory
with the origin.]

Black cultures testify that, just as there is no total, absolute, and eternal reminiscence, oblivion is also never complete. In the genealogies of their performance, the *congadeiros* rewrite and irrigate the scrolls of history and restore the person, carved from memory, who cartographs, with their harlequin(ed) Black body, with their canvas-body, the many nuances of Brazilian culture and American territories. After all, the numinousness of the voice, as *alethéa*, apparition, and the body, the domus of knowledges, confirm to our eyes and ears the course of sounds, of gestures, bringing along the beings and environments in which they are — recreating another *arkhé*, another *àṣẹ, a* mirror of another logos. As poet Edimilson vocalizes:

Família lugar

Um rio não divide
duas margens.
O que se planta nos lados
é o que separa.
. . . .
Para um devoto
tudo é muitas coisas.
Uma ravina de águas
que envolve
vivos e mortos.
. . . .
Estamos nós, os Bianos,
de enigma resolvido.
A lagoa onde somos
tem ideias de rio.

Aqui e lá são peças
dos olhos em movimento.
Como são na diferença
os mesmos Deus
e Zambiapungo.[23]

[Family Place

A river does not divide
two banks.
What is planted on the sides
is what separates them.
. . . .
For a devotee
everything is many things.
A ravine of waters
that surrounds
the living and the dead.
. . . .
We, the Bianos,
are rid of riddles.

The lagoon we are
has ideas of a river.

Here and there are parts
of eyes in motion.
As they are in their difference
the same God
and Zambiapungo.]

The memory of this knowledge is graphed, without illusory hierarchies, in the guidelines of the body and the scrolls. A knowledge embroidered like *littera* (letter) and *litura* (redaction/erasure). Engravings of voice, body, and letters turned into verse in the enchantment of chants, transcreated by me:

Envém do mar
Envém do mar
Povo de Nossa Senhora
Nossa Undamba Manganá
Envém do mar

Envém do mar

Envém do mar
Chitangome d'ingomá
Envém do mar

Envém do mar

Envém do mar
saravá povo de Zâmbi
Envém do mar

Envém do mar

Envém do mar
Vem de Congo e de Angola
de Benin e de Oiá
Envém do mar
Envém do mar

Envém do mar

povo de Nossa Senhora
de Dambi e de Dambá

de Nanã e de Oxalá
Envém do mar

Envém do mar

Envém do mar
Povo de Nossa Senhora
Nossa Undamba Manganá
Envém do mar

[Here it comes from the sea
Here it comes from the sea
People of Our Lady
Our Undamba Manganá
Here they come from the sea

Here it comes from the sea

Here it comes from the sea
Chitangome d'ingomá
Here it comes from the sea

Here it comes from the sea

Here it comes from the sea
saravá people of Nzambi
Here they come from the sea

Here it comes from the sea

Here it comes from the sea
They come from Congo and Angola
From Benin and Oya
Here it comes from the sea

Here it comes from the sea

Here it comes from the sea
people of Our Lady
of Dambi and Dambá
of Nana and Òṣàlá
Here they come from the sea

Here it comes from the sea

Here it comes from the sea
People of Our Lady
Our Undamba Manganá
Here they come from the sea]

COMPOSITION V

A CANVAS-BODY,
A FIREFLY POETICS

It is not by chance that the metamorphosis of the caterpillar and the nymph into butterfly is called imago . . . it flaps its wings. It is a matter of visual appearance and body experience at the same time. — GEORGES DIDI-HUBERMAN, *Survival of the Fireflies*

For quite some time now, Brazilian theater has been enriched by a myriad of propositions arising from several Black theater collectives, playwrights, actors, actresses, performers, directors, stage directors, and critical-theoretical perspectives most expressively focused on Blackness. Despite the diversity in terms of means of expression, all these initiatives share a common interest in diverse aspects of the historical experiences and memories of Black folks in Brazil. The elaboration of these themes, along with the dramaturgical and performing arts creations, reflects a stylistic pursuit characterized by different modes, processes, and procedures. These powerful effervescent, luminous, and instigating scenic writings challenge hegemonic, exclusionary, and stereotypical modus operandi, especially through modes and protocols of refiguration of Black people and Blackness.

Here, the ongoing practice of a Black dialogical cultural memory is actively implemented and transcreated as a recurring signifier. On scene, this signifies the continuous reactualization of various modes of perception and fabulation from

FIGURE 5.1. Denilson Tourinho, *Madam Satã. Group of the Tem* (play). Photo: Guto Munhoz, 2015.

African and African Brazilian cognitive and performative matrixes. Countless epistemologies— whether arising from the most long-lived or more recent performative collections—find expression in this dynamic process. Other contemporary poetics align themselves with this repertoire, serving as both materials and interlocutors in a fruitful experimentation, translating an emphasis on the systematic and critical inquiry into languages in the face of the staged aporias and challenges.

These artists and essayists have at their disposal an inspiring archive of information on the production of and on Black folks in several areas of knowledge, made more available on manifold digital platforms, records, documentaries, websites, theses, essays, dissertations, and reference books that make up an exemplary creative and aesthetic setting, allowing them to dynamically interact with these sources.

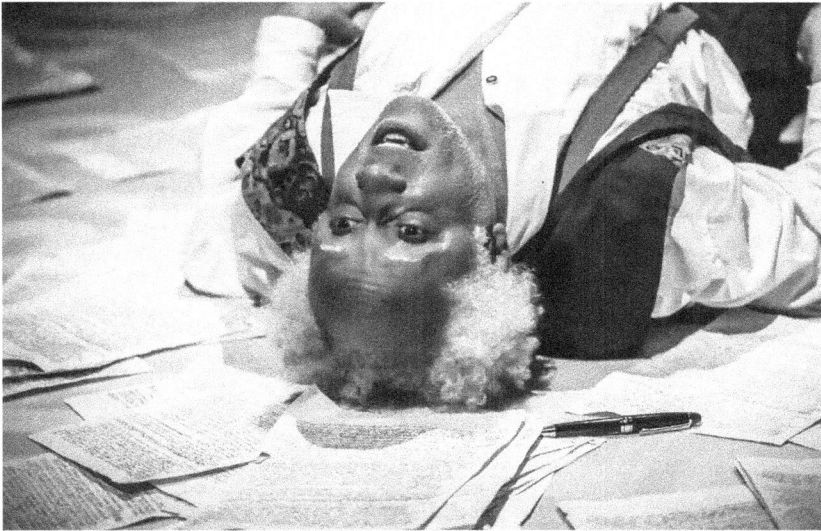

FIGURE 5.2. Hilton Cobra, *Bring Me the Head of Lima Barreto* (play, 2017).
Photo: Adeloyá OjúBará.

On theater, for instance, these archives include the historical and significant achievements of the Companhia Negra de Revistas (Black Magazine Revue Company), created by De Chocolat; the Teatro Experimental do Negro (Black Experimental Theater), designed by Abdias Nascimento and D. Maria do Nascimento; the Balé Brasiliana (Brasiliana Ballet), cofounded by Haroldo Costa; the Teatro Popular (Popular Theater), by Solano Trindade; the scenography of Santa Rosa; the Companhia Testa (Testa Company), created in 1975 by Nivalda Costa, a Black director, actress, and playwright; as well as more recent productions, such as those of the already famous Bando de Teatro Olodum (Olodum Theater Group), among numerous other initiatives, equally outstanding and masterful.

On stage, talented actors and actresses shine, following the legacy and the acting paths expanded by Arinda Serafim, Grande Otelo, Léa Garcia, Milton Gonçalves, Nélson Xavier, Chica Xavier, Zezé Motta, Mário Gusmão, Antônio Pitanga, Antônio Pompeu, Hilton Cobra, Cyda Moreno, among many others, including the talents of the new generations, who are already imperative references in this scenario, and synonymous with remarkable authorial mastery. In the arts of dance, already renowned dancers such as Zebrinha, Carmen Luz, Rui Moreira, Inaicyra Falcão, Júnia Bertolino, Evandro Passos, and many others, longevous ones and younger ones, walk the path paved by Mercedes Souza, Marlene Silva, and De Chocolat, inspiring new generations of dancers.

Also in the realm of visual and digital arts, cinema and video, remarkable achievements by Emanoel Araújo, Jorge dos Anjos, Rosana Paulino, Zózimo Bulbul, and Joel Zito Araújo are noteworthy. In literature, beyond the more classic Black canon, populated by writers of the highest historical competence and importance,[1] contemporary authors from different generations stand out in inspiring poetic and fictional creations. Works like *Um defeito de cor*, by Ana Maria Gonçalves, demonstrate a sophisticated narrative, both in the mastery of the complex aesthetic elaboration of the many utterances and themes that the novel invokes and installs, in the multiple perspectives of narration, as well as in the complex articulation of narrated voices that revisit multiple genres and textualities.

In all areas of creation, these collections multiply. And with all these materials, the contemporary Black scene is fermented and seasoned, expanding the focus of Blackness, as aesthetic possibility, invocation, and epistemic system.

A diverse content inhabits and circumscribes these dramaturgies and scenic practices, in their different perspectives. Here reigns a resounding postural voice that challenges the pedagogies of systematic absence and exclusion, unveiling the ingenious methods, apparatuses, and structuring systems of racism and their recurrent sanctions. Simultaneously, this voice celebrates the numerous achievements of Black peoples, highlighting their fundamental and constitutive role in Brazilian culture and society and reaffirming their historical relevance.

Concerning this vibrant theatrical scene, Salloma Salomão offers the following insight:

> What has been being watched and appreciated is a multifaceted Black theatricality, loaded with political contents addressing class, race, and gender relations. At the same time, these relations have been crossed by resignified and actualized African civilizing values, along with the modern reconfiguration of Afrodiasporic imagery into texts and bodies. These micro-stories and fictions are also fragmentary and almost always incomplete, unfinished abstract constructs, designed to undermine and interdict prevailing—albeit fractured, yet enduring—narratives that uphold the centrality, superiority, and uniqueness of the Western, Christian, white, heteronormative, and male gaze. Primarily, they are, above all, diverse explorations of the self-construction of Black women, the genocide of the Black youth, the microcracks of interpersonal and structural racism, and the profound effects wrought by subjectivities plagued by racial inequality and misogyny.[2]

These actions undoubtedly produce effects of displacement and estrangement that necessarily affect the audience's reception as they are confronted with unfamiliar experiences regarding the protocols and scope of representations and appearances of Black people in the Brazilian stage. The exercise of reflection is brought about by many plays, as stated by Lucélia Sérgio: "In these shows, one can discern a quest, drawing from diverse sources of theoretical, dramaturgical research, and scenic experimentation, to find expressive forms that account for the subjects and aesthetics on the agenda of each group."[3]

Salomão also emphasizes this point: "What can be seen, in addition to the struggle for existence in a traditionally white and privileged space, is the continuous quest for sophisticated sound, visual, graphic, imagistic, choreographic, poetic, and bodily symbologies rooted in Black African heritage. Elements of the Black musical show combined with contents that can be termed as decolonial post-dramatic theatricalities, uniquely applied to ethnic-racial contexts."[4] The conflict of ideas sparks controversy, reactions, and urgencies, heating up discussions and reflections, as astutely observed by playwright and director Eugênio Lima:

> I also see that Black aesthetics and its poetics are subjects under discussion. However, at the same time, there seems to be a considerable reaction to this, as if it were still an exception, as if this debate was confined to a niche, rather than a debate that should influence the broader landscape of theater-making. While there is much talk about Black theater, there is a noticeable silence concerning the overwhelming majority of groups that remain exclusively white. . . . We find ourselves in the midst of a robust confrontation, where several groups are engaged in diverse and well-organized endeavors—each exhibiting significant power and poetic expressions. Legítima Defesa is an integral part of this ongoing historical process, which has not started and certainly will not end with us.[5]

This urgent debate is also manifested in the body of work (plays and essays) by Aldri Anunciação, presenting a scenic and theoretical proposition he calls "Dramaturgia do Debate" (Dramaturgy of the debate). In his aesthetic approach, Anunciação introduces "a clash between collective forces instead of a clash between encapsulated subjectivities," striving to forge a "potential poetic of dissent,"[6] as well as "to shift readers' thoughts (regardless of their ethnic/phenotypic predominance) and to stimulate sensations related to the social issues in Brazil." The author also seeks to provide "the audience with a dramaturgy that brings to the scenic debate the identity conflict of a multiple subject and the positive and negative consequences of the (analog and digital) diasporic transits that produced (and still produce) diffuse identities."[7]

A compelling drive and leitmotif of rupture, coupled with simultaneous intervention in the status quo, can be observed in these achievements. This allows us to draw parallels with the strategies of the so-called Theater of the Real—a pioneering performance movement, which is not to be confused with the realist and naturalist aesthetics of the nineteenth century—an innovative performance movement influenced by a sui generis thought of intervention and reshaping of the scene, as Martin notes, "revealing something has become as important as changing something."[8] In the Theater of the Real, memory, recreated through various scenic devices and enunciation strategies, is employed "to form pictures, construct cases, make arguments, create historic ruptures, and situate the spectators in history."[9] Departing from dramaturgical models and conventions, these performance practices provide us with a foundation to "understand personal, social, and political phenomena by means of aesthetic invention, intervention, and implementation."[10]

The propositions evoked here follow these systematic paths of interventions and contraventions, as one can observe, for instance, in the play *Alguma coisa a ver com uma missão* (Something to do with a mission), where the Cia Os Crespos theater company investigates "the spheres of relations amidst racial insurrection, historical repression, and contemporary racism in order to comprehend the subversive movements of Black populations. These movements have played a transformative role in racial sociability and were faced with the conservative counter-revolution movement and the entrenched social roles and myths that perpetuate values from our past of slavery."[11]

The experimentation with transdisciplinary and transversal languages reveals attitudes toward and shifts in aesthetic-ethical protocols and values. Within these poetics, Black embodied practices emerge as theoretical, conceptual, and performative foundations—an epistemic system that fecundates the scenes, expanding the scopes of the body as a locus and environment for the production and registration of knowledge, memory, affections, and actions. A thought-body.

The body, implemented and constituted in this manner, turns into a canvas-body, an image-body, an archive interwoven with a network of allusions and a repertoire of stimuli and arguments, translating a distinct geopolitics of the body: a polis body, a body of temporalities and spatialities, the gentrified body, the witness-body, and the body of records. It is a historically connoted body, which personifies the voices that denounce and name the itinerary of violence of our daily lives, tirelessly carving out alternate paths for another existence—one that is fuller and fairer. A body/voice inventory that cleans, rebuilds, restores, reclaims, inhales, and exhales, in an enduring healing process, digging out alternate paths of other possible becomings, always yearning for transformations within the social corpus.

A political body that speaks for itself, the herald of what remains unspoken or not repeated—because it was interdicted, censored, excluded; a herald of what remained implicit, hidden, unmentioned, undeclared, avoided; a herald of that which was not enunciated, not pronounced, not uttered, and which was imposed like a terrifying silence. Another embodied practice interposes the interdiction and the pedagogy of absence and exclusion. An embodied practice that argues, postulates, proposes, and expresses. A biographeme body,[12] weaving lived experiences with imagination, crafting its own autofiction—a body whose utterance performs a "personalized voice" that, as Zumthor suggests, "resacralizes the unholy itinerary of existence."[13]

The canvas-body, a cultural corpus, in its varied range, adherence, and multiple profiles, becomes a locus and a privileged environment for a myriad of poetics intertwined in the aesthetic making. This *gesta* is elaborated through scenic creations inspired by poetics of visualities, spatialities, luminosities, sonorities, subjectivities, and dramaturgies that experiment with alliances between technologies and rituals.

Images are, as Samain postulates,[14] thinking forms. Within them, the most complex knowledges are enacted and disseminated. Thus, they affect and implicate us, for, as thought, images produce something about what or who they represent, but significantly also bring "the thought of the one who produced the photograph, the painting, the drawing," along with the thoughts of all of those who have gazed upon these depictions. All these spectators who "incorporated their thoughts, their fantasies, their delusions, and even their sometimes deliberate interventions" in them.[15]

There are too many distorted images of Black people, Blackness, and Black culture. Caricatural, biased, and demeaning, these figurations compromised the very dignity of those portrayed, even abolishing their human nature, their humanity. These deceptive images, as Edimilson Pereira de Almeida refers to them, persist in portraying a distorted body and a threatening subject.[16] Even today, these perverse depictions appear in narratives and in *flashes*, across countless representational means, stages, platforms, and devices.

These grotesque and atrocious images serve as reminders of the iron muzzle —an instrument of torture and a tool for imposing silence. It stands as a metaphor for the violence and oppression endured by enslaved Black folks, a mask mentioned with sharp irony and sarcasm by Machado de Assis:

> Like many other social institutions, slavery brought with it certain trades and implements. I will mention only a few of those implements because of their connection with a particular trade. There was the neck iron, the leg

iron, and the iron muzzle. . . . It had only three holes, two to see through and one to breathe through, and it was fastened at the back of the head with a padlock. . . . The muzzle was a grotesque thing, but then human and social order cannot always be achieved without the grotesque or, indeed, without occasional acts of cruelty. The tinsmiths would hang them up at the doors of their shops. But that's enough of muzzles for the moment.[17]

The image "participates in stories and memories which precede it, from which it feeds before being reborn one day, before reappearing now in my *hic et nunc*."[18] However, the thought of images often hesitates to reveal many of their historical motivations and methodologies. Thus, it is not only crucial to expose the harmful effects of images, but imperative to dismantle them, interrupt their flow, to affect them, and propose other possibilities for their production and recording.

As Martin cautions us, artists imbued with a critical stance, operating within an aesthetic that also seeks revelation, believe that "subject matter cannot be transparent if the methods used to present it are opaque. They show their spectators some of the complex ways the relationship between theater and life can be conceptualized, performed, and reperformed. The question is not only what happens to history when it is made into art, but what happens to art when it makes history."[19] Now, we may ask ourselves: Which knowledges do the images of Black folks and Blackness proposed by Black scenes reveal or propose? What do these images think?

One potent avenue for not just denouncing the system, but mainly affecting, disrupting, and transforming it is through strategic interventions that challenge and dismantle the ploys of decayed and distorted figurations, as does Grace Passô: "Theater, for me, is some sort of '*aquilombamento*.'"[20] A *quilombo* is a space of resistance and also a space for strengthening ourselves among our people. All this to say that the theater I understand, what I do, is more connected to a certain social craft; it is more connected to the space of the market than to the space of the mall. What I do is more connected to the body, to the idea of a meeting for a few people, full of risks."[21] As Passô writes elsewhere, "In the theater, I gravitate toward creative functions because I like them, but also to create space for myself. A considerable part of art in Brazil is very elitist and ends up dealing with bodies in an elitist way as well. Getting closer to the conceptual functions allowed me to create a space to fully exist in a way that resonates with that I believe."[22]

In this field, the images of Black people transcend fixed or unitary parameters; they are mutable and kinesthetic.

Within the propositions of the Black art scene, particularly in Black theater, in general, there is a noticeable shift concerning the compositional modes

FIGURE 5.3. *Black* (play, Companhia Brasileira de Teatro, 2017). *From left to right:* Cátia Damasceno, Felipe Soares, and Grace Passô.

of identities and personas. It involves a retreat or refusal of the traditional mimetic notion of representation, especially those fixed, stable, and framed representations, in favor of increasingly fluid and relational identities, allowing for more mobility, dynamism, and transient fabulations, particularly those concerning affectional, gender, and sexual orientations, in constant flux, always in transit and migrating. They are woven together by biographemes and autofictions, playfully challenging the notion of the shattered and sacrificial subject of Western modernity, which is already crumbling. As observed by Saturnino: "For Merleau-Ponty . . . 'I don't merely have a body, my body is me.' The subjective body is not merely a thing, an object, but rather a permanent condition of experience, a perceptive openness to the world. The expanded, prosthetic, and altered body . . . lies beyond the binary dialectic, complexifying the issue of the visibility and divisibility of the subject."[23] According to Fischer-Lichte, between the order of representation, where "everything that is perceived is done with reference to a particular fictional character,"[24] and the order of presence, where "The actor's body is perceived in its phenomenality, as his [*sic*] particular being-in-the-world," performances produce variations of displacements that "seek to destabilize the audience's gaze, taking us out of the comfort zone of predictable relationships and throwing us into multiple states of instability."[25] The tension between the real and the fictional becomes, thus, as the same author notes, "principles of performativity." These interfaces enhance the personal motivations of the audience, causing effects of proximity and memory in the interaction between performers and actors, triggering an intense relationship between the performer and the spectator, sometimes turned into a "specta(c) tor," as Boal wrote.[26]

Aldri Anunciação, for instance, invests in allegorical types in constant transit, problematizing their historically and aesthetically constitutive personhoods and identities. By placing his characters in scenes-spaces of confinement, the author aims "to dramaturgically organize a (semantic) disorder of identity," fostering "a clash between collective forces instead of a clash between encapsulated subjectivities."[27]

In Marcio Abreu's dramaturgy, we encounter subjects pushing the unexplored limits of a body without organs, à la Artaud.[28] These characters inquire into the very ruins of their subjectivities, stripping away aggregated, conditioned, recurrent signifiers. Escaping from the common articulations and nexuses of conventional representations and fabulations, these personas navigate the risk-laden space between being and the possibility of not being, between pain and joy. They engage in exercises of self-translation and postponed exchanges, pushing the limits of creation and revitalization in their provisional autofictions and their fragments of subjectivities, alternating between fugitive states, quests, divergences, pretenses, and indetermination.

This body under debate and in dispute is often inspired by the repertoires of ancestrality as a possibility of social and aesthetic refoundation. This is exemplified in Adriana Paixão's testimonies about *As Capulanas*: "*Capulanas* is deeply anchored in Black aesthetics, recontextualizing and reframing religious elements of jongos, candomblés, and umbandas for the urban spectacle. Memories of African ancestrality and the diasporic Black body play pivotal roles in the group's theatrical scene and shape, together with other symbolic elements, its specific cultural and philosophical dimensions."[29]

The refigured and whole body is also highlighted by Lucélia Sérgio, as she approaches several current productions, including *Quando Efé* (When Efé), a dance performance by Cia. Fusion, from Belo Horizonte:

In this production, hip hop coexists with *moda de viola*, urban dances with the Congado, and electronic beats with the *tambores de mineiros* [Mineiros drums]. The influence of one over the other is undeniable, manifesting in a hybrid body that speaks to belonging, the construction of living memory, and a contemporary identity. In the inquiry of young Black male identities, the boys of *Quando efé* do not speak of the slave ship, slavery, or pain—influential elements in the process of identity construction. Instead, their narrated testimony revolves around celebration, the land, the music, the landscape changed by their footsteps, [the testimony is about] a molded and sculpted body, an account of belonging rather than rejection. What unfolds are Black bodies with a place in the world. Conflicts/scenic games complement the identity and set up an experience of self-contemplation.[30]

Along this path of countless rehearsals and experiments, the canvas-body is also transfigured into a feminine body of Blackness. A remarkable number of women playwrights, actresses, directors, and performers bring the body to the stage as locus of creation of an alternate knowledge about women, particularly Black women. They figure the body as the inscription canvas of a desired recomposition of woman. The theatrical tradition and its rhetorical-ideological apparatuses are challenged through the lens of these women authors, who craft and reshape Brazilian theater's familiar itineraries, instilling and spreading energizing dysrhythmia and dissonance into and on it.

These women are many.

In the 1990s, a wave of texts written by women emerged in Brazilian literature. In these works, the fictional and poetic text assumed a pivotal role as a potent instrument for a compelling erasure, discontinuity, and deconstruction of the countless and constant negative figurations of women characters. It became a powerful means for articulating a voice against the racism and sexism embedded in oblique discursive practices.[31] In a 1995 statement, Miriam Alves referred to the Black woman's literary production at that time:

> The racism of the whites against Black people and the sexism of men against women are similar. . . . In general, the Black woman writers' inclination is to engage in the struggle of men, which is called universal struggle. The specificity of being a woman writer that is blossoming in her work goes unnoticed. . . . There's no need to be talking about the whip, about slavery, in order to write Black literature. Art is freedom, liberation. My art is deeply entwined with who I am. And who am I? I am Black, I am a woman, a single mother, a businesswoman, a daughter, a worker, an activist. . . . If I am unable to convey my message in a short story, I'll attempt to do so in a poem. Should poetry fall short, I'll turn to a tale. If even that proves inadequate, I'll try a novel, and, who knows, maybe a comic book

will do? These are my mediums. Literature is my tool. If I can communicate by filling pages with commas, and if the reader can grasp that I am speaking from the very fabric of Brazil, where it is settled, from the [situation of] misery in which the Black population finds itself, then I will fill those pages with commas.[32]

In the twenty-first century, these theatrical interventions have become notable. In her performance *Como falar de coisas invisíveis* (How to talk about invisible things), Val Souza captivates the audience by initiating direct eye contact and posing a recurring question: "I am a Black woman. Do you hear me? Can you listen to me?"[33] This distinction between hearing and listening emphasizes and establishes an urgency: Is the Black woman, the Black person, truly heard, or do they still remain irrelevant to those who pretend to see and hear them without actually perceiving and listening to them?

As the audience faces direct questioning, a subtle discomfort arises, leading to responses that oscillate between reticence and eloquence. In this dynamic, the audience becomes an integral part of the performer's contemplation. Throughout the performance, Souza's penetrating gaze and voice persist in triggering this questioning and inquiry, adopting a playful, appealing, and sometimes interpellating approach. The result is a thought-provoking and interactive experience that demands reflection and active participation from the audience.

In *Dramaturgias do front* (Front dramaturgies) and other plays, through experiences with multiple theater experimental languages, Dione Carlos fabulates a woman's body of minimal lines and profiles. She portrays the woman as a subject in photograms and silhouettes that move within a spatiality more enriched by vocalizations than by tangible figurations; by doing so, Dione Carlos sets up each speech and gesture of utterance as vocal scores, adopting a compositional grammar that excels for its unexpected arguments and for escaping causality and linear progression. Her scenes are composed by asymmetric groupings that sew together the patches of everyday life, avoiding conventional syntaxes and monolithic figuration. Her texts are intricate tapestries woven with fragments of subjectivities in a constant process of subtle recompositions or decompositions, as photograms arranged in a mosaic technique, which are aligned whether by dispersion or condensation, affecting the ordering of what is narrated. The challenge for spectators lies and imposes itself both in relation to the utterances and the devices and modes employed in their enunciative and narrative construction.

In her dramaturgy, including her *Manifesta cabocla* (Cabocla manifesto), the significant *I*, as a *shifter*, translates the movement and the resignifying transit of the woman-*I* who rules enunciation. This strategy that interconnects the *I* with *she* and other(s) (shes), turning *she* into a collective dimension, a body of shared affections that rules enunciation, embraced by the projection of a consonant *we*.

This *she*, known by multiple names, "walks through many places: forests, cities, villages, *quilombos, terreiros, favelas, pelourinhos*,[34] theaters, barracoons, street parties, universities, balls, alleys," desiring "living bodies and open spaces," for her "greatest instrument is, in fact, the body." The body itself, in turn, serves as a repertoire of ancestral memory that shelters spiral temporality, in which lays—with intensity—a synchronicity of voices that, as a chorus, repeats aphorisms such as: "A voice can never be given, nor lent, or represented to or by someone. A voice can only be amplified." This idea can also be expressed more extensively: "I see seeds hidden by mothers in their daughter's braids / —Urucum on their skin on celebration days, black genipap on war victories celebrations. / —The blessings of black hands in prayers to fight *quebrantos*.[35] / —The crowns, the headdresses, the headcloths, the rosary beads, *panos da costa*, the pilgrimages, the aroma of palm oil, the candles lit at baptisms and funerals, the prayers and lamentations, basil baths, the popcorn that cleanses the body."[36] In this process of (affective) investment, the journey of self-recognition is consistently inaugural and alchemical, involving a continuous "transformation of silence into language and action."[37] This is a mark, for example, of the performance *Bombril*, by Priscila Rezende, which can also be seen in other works by the same artist, in which she utilizes her hair as a device, shaping a modus operandi that seeks to transform the systems of representation of Black women. By doing so, she sets up a powerful aesthetic and social intervention that unfolds within urban spaces and their outskirts.

In these new cartographies of women, younger generations draw inspiration from ancestral poetics, actively claiming, honoring and restoring them, as Stephanie Ribeiro reveals in this emblematic and uplifting assessment of the *Tombamento Generation*:

> This generation of Black youth, tired of the aesthetical invisibility and the condemnation of their physical features, deemed negative by a racist society, chose to reject mainstream standards. They recreated their own aesthetical definitions. They slayed. The box braids, common amongst Black matriarchs, became multicolored. Turbans, often worn by grandmothers and mothers working as "the help," gained colors and patterns as they became accessories to go to the club. Hair, once a big problem in their childhoods, is now seen as a solution. The *Tombamento* Generation is a fusion of ancestrality affirmation with the (re)creation of historic possibilities.[38]

Throughout these processes, Grace Passô's work has also been emblematic and transgressive:

> What does it mean to be a Black actress in Brazil? It is exactly the same as being a Black woman in Brazil. The prevailing social imaginary imposes an extremely limiting frame in Brazilian cinema for people like me, reflecting the country's deeply ingrained structural racism. For a long time, whether on television or in cinema, I have always been invited to play the same characters, always related to subservience. And I'm not talking about their professions. The point is that these characters, when written through a non-Black gaze, are generally subservient to the plot: women who do not love, or who are the size of white conscience when it comes to the racism they experience. Very early on, I learned to try to shield myself from that gaze, which is kind of what Black women do. No wonder I started writing as a means of self-protection.[39]

In the geography of the woman's body, envisioned as an agenda for the inscription of intimate knowledge, the self-image, imbued with a rich marker of vocality, photographs itself. The movement of this self, the subject of its own enunciation, impregnates the text with prefacing references, citing the woman's body as an ever-renewed landscape shaped by herself and her women predecessors. It is through and by means of body language, the object of inquiry, that journeys are accomplished, for metamorphoses take place in this crossing. The body, in a continuous process of displacement and resignification, becomes itself geography, landscape of pronunciations and utterances, territory of pronounced words, endless continent pierced by polyphonies and melopoeias. A body engaged in a perpetual healing process, as expanded through the voice of Val Souza: "Health is contemplating existence comprehensively. I no longer wish to think about fragmentation because it leads me to give excessive importance to illness. I aim to foster health for bodies like mine."[40]

A voice that not only heals but also cuts with its sharpness, as actress and poet Elisa Lucinda playfully expounds:

> *Moço, cuidado com ela . . .*
> *Cuidado com cada letra que manda pra ela!*
> *Tá acostumada a viver por dentro,*
> *transforma fato em elemento*
> *a tudo refoga, ferve, frita*
> *ainda sangra tudo no próximo mês.*[41]

[Mister, watch out for her . . .
Careful with every letter you send her!
She's used to living inside,
she turns facts into elements
she braises, boils, fries everything
and the next month she bleeds out all of it.]

According to Collins, "this journey toward self-definition has political significance," for it "offers a powerful challenge to the externally defined, controlling
images of African American women." [42] This *I-we*,[43] restored in its predicates
and affections, can now joyfully love and offer themself to the other, as poet
Geni Guimarães writes:

Tanto sangrou para não sangrar
tanto fez para desfazer
tanto aspirou
cuspiu
bebeu
se deu, lutou
que ao se vencer, se amou.

Hoje exibe a negra bela cara
ao sol ardente que reveste a rua.
Satisfaz-se.
A vida é uma cabeça.
A consciência é sua.[44]

[Bled so much not to bleed
Done so much to undo
aspired so much
spat
drank
given, fought
that by overcoming herself, she loved herself.

Now, showing her pretty Black face
to the burning sun that covers the street.
Self-satisfied.
Life is a head.
Conscience is yours.]

FIGURE 5.4. Priscila Rezende, *Bombril* (performance). Photo: Priscila Rezende. Courtesy of the artist, 2010.

Black theater accesses double qualities and attributes of image composition—polychromatic and polyrhythmic designs—that (re)shape poetics of luminosities and powerful sonorities.

The visual realm is one of the most powerful gateways to images. No wonder the ancient Greeks referred to the eyes as windows of the soul, as noted by Bosi: "The image, whether mental or inscribed, engages in a dual relationship with the visible, as vividly illustrated by the verbs *appear* and *seem*.[45] The object is presented, it appears, it is open (Latin: *apparet*) to the vision, it surrenders to us as an *appearance*: this is the primordial imago that we have of it. Subsequently, with the reproduction of the appearance, the latter *seems* like what appeared to us. From appearance to resemblance: these contiguous moments are closely held by language."[46] Visually, a striking stylistic feature of these dramaturgies and scenes hints at a composition technique I refer to as "rhetoric of patchwork." In this approach, objects, figures, and themes are elaborated from remnants, patches, and fragments of everyday life, patched together in a score that, much like a tapestry, excels by its juxtaposition of contrasts, colors, drawings, and tracings that may appear uneven and misaligned, resembling an arabesque fabric manufactured by a customary ritual of incorporating diverse elements, akin to a hieroglyphic inscription.

In this aesthetic of flaps—a yo-yo patchwork technique, a way of symbolically and literally weaving and sewing—the body is presented painted with wisdoms. Similarly to what happens in Black ritual practices, both religious and secular, movements, voice, choreographies, language properties, costumes, skin drawings, and hair designs stylistically and metonymically trace this body/corpus as a locus and environment of wisdom and memory, literally making the body's surface a text and the subject a sign, interpreter and interpretant, simultaneously.

These poetics embrace the most diverse chromaticism, both in skin languages and scenographic compositions. Noteworthy is the refinement and synesthetic sophistication of the scenographies, as well as the designs and plays of lights. This polychromy produces brilliant and stellar luminosities, forming an explosion of scenic plasticity—an African technique par excellence, in which the use of puerile materials, recycled and reinvented remnants, are arranged in syntaxes that produce sensory, perceptive, and expressive effects. The designs, light shows, and colors are structuring elements, even in the minimalist scenographies that explore gaps and voids, and in the aesthetics of shades projected by faint and opaque luminosities.

See, for example, the scenic plasticity of several productions by Bando de Teatro Olodum, Companhia dos Comuns, Os Crespos, Caixa Preta, Coletivo de Mulheres Negras from Belo Horizonte, Capulanas Cia de Arte Negra, Coletivo Em Legítima Defesa, as well as the opera *Pretoperitamar*, featuring Anelis Assumpção as the musical director.

But the image is not confined to the sensory landscapes of visibility; it can also be composed by a quality of sound that requires attentive listening, revealing itself to us through its auditory quality. In the multifaceted realm of Black aesthetic and its diverse properties, these stylistically convergent and complementary possible qualities of images, both visual and auditory, draw close to each other, for, in this realm, the image can manifest not only through visual forms but also through sound.

Combining visual and sound tonus, this body of bright visualities is infused with sonorities. The canvas-body becomes then a voiced body, in which the said, the unsaid, and the re-said is a significant axiom, an emanation. The use of the voice is, thus, instrumental, for it creates—in the production processes and techniques of phonic languages—multiple vocal engravings. The sonorities' vocal scores and rhythms are composed of multiple emission resources, encompassing minimum syllables, onomatopoeia, cooing, lullabies, solfeggios, and more extended phrasings. In these expressive pronunciations and rhythms, the word incarnates the body, it vibrates in the choreography of gestures, it lends voice to silence. As Zumthor asserts, "That which provides room to speaking, that through which the word is articulated, is a double desire: that of saying, and that which gives back the content of the uttered words."[47]

Here I recall the performances of poet and visual artist Ricardo Aleixo. With a keen aesthetic perception, Aleixo combines elements of concrete poetry with the rhythmic patterns of African Brazilian matrixes in his presentations. The artist crafts an ambience and a *verbivocomusical* (verbal-vocal-musical) poiesis in which polyrhythmic, multivocal, synesthetic, and kinesthetic constructions par excellence prevail. A poetics that employs sampling, composition, sound and image filtering, as well as rhythmic objects, some handcrafted or everyday items, resulting in an eloquent and fascinating sonority.

Similarly, Grace Passô's performances showcase her exploration of vocal techniques, where she sings vibratos, challenging the boundaries of vocal expression. Her vocalizations include speech, silences, screams, cooing, chants, gestures, laments, noises, interjections; sharp, rasping, poignant phrases; vocalizations, and multiple sonorities in her body, as we can enjoy in her outstanding performances in *Preto* (Black) and *Vaga carne* (Vacant flesh), for example.

In *Outras rosas* (Other roses), a play by Anderson Feliciano, Soraya Martins engages in a remarkable and subtle exploration of voice postulations and intonations. She repeats a single and emblematic phrase, "I don't think I should have to get up," 360 times. This repetition evokes the defiant attitude of Rosa Parks, the Black woman who, in 1955 in Montgomery, Alabama, refused to give up her bus seat to a white passenger, challenging the apartheid rules in the United States. By bringing Parks's figure to the present day, the play somehow denounces the urgency of attitudes to challenge the enduring structures and modus operandi of racism. This innovative approach, both in terms of the text and performance, stands as a powerful means to confront and challenge the status quo.

In many of the previously mentioned scenic arrangements and scores, it becomes evident that the images are granulated by high levels of vocality and visuality, establishing—without succumbing to illusionary and fragile dichotomies— a mirroring game between seeing and hearing, vision and listening. These aspects intermingle, alternate, or reflect in the sonic achievement, as well as in their similarities and kinship.

These alignments claim gesture and dance as expressive and significant tools. In many of these performances, movements engrave the voice into the air, drawing and sculpting silhouettes, sculptures, and sound visualizations in scenic spatialities, turning gestures into a system of iconicity that frames the aesthetic style.

In this aesthetic, gestures assume an exemplary role, as a constitutive in-itself of performance, being itself a performative synthesis. Thus, movements and gestures inhabit a place that is, at the very least, dual and simultaneous: They are equivalent to something that semantically and mimetically evokes—even if peripherally, in a complementary or supplementary manner—a word, a sound, an image. Likewise, they obliquely occupy all senses, spaces, and times in the realm of their own realization, forming a totalizing synthesis. Beyond any desire for representation, this synthesis configures an act, also translating, by extension, drama itself, as tension, friction, and conflict. In the first case, gestures are performed analogically, whereas in the second, they are mainly materialized through contiguity. According to Zumthor: "The 'pure' form of the oral poetic work is what, from the dimension given to its space by gesture, subsists in memory, after words have been suppressed. Such is the aesthetic experience that constitutes performance.... The gesture demandingly recreates a sacred spacetime. The personalized voice emphasizes the profane itinerary of existence."[48]

For Galard, gestures are "the poetry of the act."[49] As poiesis of movement and as minimal forms, gestures might evoke the fullest senses. For Paul Zumthor, gestures of the face (expression and mime), gestures of the upper limbs, gestures of the head, gestures of the torso, and gestures of the entire body, when together, "carry meaning in the form of hieroglyphic writing."[50]

The signifying qualities of African-inspired gestures become a powerful expressive code as a scenic element, forming a constitutive part of the aesthetic languages of Black performances. From Porto Alegre, Rio Grande do Sul, the Caixa Preta group, like many others, uses "African Brazilian aesthetic elements as scenic procedures in the service of narrative and staging." In the premiere staging of *Hamlet sincrético* in 2005, "African Brazilian gestures are transformed into a scenic code full of meaning and artistic power."[51]

By integrating scenic languages and codes, gestures intricately draw the body into adorned spatialities. This walking body, expanded and highlighted in and by spatialities, walks, rests, runs—always engaging in migrations that perform an occupation, whether literal or symbolic, of places and non-places. This implementation of *aquilombamentos* reterritorializes spaces, turning them into an expressive component of scenic movements and wanderings.

Cidade Vodu (Voodoo City), written and directed by José Fernando de Azevedo in collaboration with the group Teatro de Narradores (Theater of Narrators), from São Paulo and staged for the first time at MITsp (Mostra Internacional de Teatro de São Paulo) in 2016, takes the audience on a journey through a ruined and decomposing scenic spatiality that mirrors the imbalances and series of inquiries that scrutinize the geographies of public and private spaces, the plight of immigrants in São Paulo, and the geopolitical relations between Brazil and Haiti. Using an apparatus of technological, visual, and sound devices, *Cidade Vodu* composes a compelling narrative mediated by key narrators who create zones of discomfort, heightening the audience's perception and critical emotions.

As well analyzed by Rafael Villas Bôas, in *Cidade Vodu*:

> Throughout the play, the Brazilian audience is constantly placed under layers of tension: are we the victims or beneficiaries of progress? Do we see the scene from the deck or the hold of the slave ship?.... Leaving the conventional theatrical apparatus.... the Narradores chose *vila Itororó*—a building complex from the early 20th century that occupies the space of an entire block, now in ruins and under the possession of São Paulo City—as the setting for the production. From which stance do we watch the narrative?... The initial movement of the play unfolds at the external side of the space, on the street, where actors wearing military clothing and blue berets, in allusion to the military troops who serve in UN missions, guide the audience.... Throughout this journey, participants wear headphones, listening to a narration detailing the process of the slave trade from Africa to the American continent, with richness of detail about the cruel actions committed by pirate traffickers and their subordinates. The borders of the great buildings, surrounding the horizon, grow around us; with the contrast established by the narration, these buildings now appear as a result of the blood and sweat of the working class.... The atmosphere of containment and control is permanent: throughout this journey, we are accompanied, watched, and restrained by the ones wearing blue berets.[52]

In *Antônia*, an adaptation of *Antigone*, carried out through streets and alleys of Salvador, Bahia, Sanara Rocha, the director and protagonist of the production, appropriates and resignifies locations in Salvador. This scenic procession rearranges the pathways of Black people through usually hostile urban routes, where violence against Black folks is prevalent. It becomes an occupation of public spaces, resignifying them with a creative scenic action that is simultaneously politically and ideologically provocative, as highlighted by Gustavo Melo Cerqueira:

> Firstly, public spaces, such as the streets, are potentially violent spaces for Black bodies, often perceived as suspicious or threatening—in the case of men—or accessible and violable—in the case of women. In some ways,

in public spaces, the Black body, as scholar Frank B. Wilkerson puts it, "magnetically attracts bullets." . . . Secondly, it is crucial to recognize that, while staging *Antônia* on the street, the public space itself was invoked as the scenario of the production, actively involving the audience in the narrative. This engagement is reinforced by the racial identification between the cast, and the audience emphasized during the presentation.[53]

In the project that resulted in the production *Alguma coisa a ver com uma missão* (Something to do with a mission), Os Crespos aim to "intervene in the everyday life of the city, engaging with the public space. During the initial phase of this research, the group presented, in different locations of the city, the interventions *Ninhos e revides — Mirando o Haiti* (Nests and retaliations — targeting Haiti) and *De brasa e pólvora* (On embers and gunpowder). These interventions laid the groundwork for *Alguma coisa a ver com uma missão*, which leads the public to learn the history of Black struggles for freedom." Through the journey of two Black women, Os Crespos "take the audience on a journey that dates back to the Black revolts and uprisings that were responsible for securing our freedom and are symbols of our people's resistance. The production draws inspiration from Bantu musicality, enabling the creation of songs and arrangements for some original *vissungos*. Musicians accompany both the audience and the actors along the way."[54] We can also highlight other language apparatuses, such as the production *Quaseilhas*, which also displaces the audience through the unique use of the Yoruba language throughout the performance. This expands the discontinuous spatial displacement installed as performative islands that intersect and relate, forming an archipelago, echoing Glissant's poetics of diversity.[55] The use of a foreign language induces a sense of estrangement in the spectator, who becomes dispossessed themself. It requires attention and effort to absorb the narrative that is not easily grasped, despite being evoked by a strong visual and sound imagery. The spectator, in their discomfort, must function as a translator navigating areas of uncertainty and zones of instability, confronted by their own otherness in the face of the linguistic code that estranges, disturbs, and disconcerts them. This demands new resources to establish other possible perspectives of communication and connection with the narrative, by means of a translation that, more than verbal, must be intersemiotic.

This theme of—often forced—transit and migration is a significant element of *Buraquinhos* (Little holes), a play by Jhonny Salaberg, which immerses the audience in a wandering journey through spatialities and threatening and hostile environments, where a teenager tries to escape a wrongful accusation of theft, leading to a desperate and frantic flight. The protagonist, still a child, traverses a path marked by hopes and despair, embarking on an agonizing journey through the territories and open veins of Latin America, until he is finally reduced to a bloody heart, delivered to a grieving mother.

Similarly, *Violento* (Violent), written by Alexandre de Sena and Preto Amparo and performed by Preto Amparo, initiates the narrative in the vicinity of the theater, that is, at the public space, where the character is tied with a string to a police car toy that chases him through the streets amid the sound of a blaring siren. This chase serves as a potent metaphor—an antagonist tied to the Black person—akin to *Buraquinhos*, depicting institutionalized violence and structural racism against the Black individual.

Here, I also think of the constitution of spaces that reclaim places, buildings, settling urban *aquilombamentos*, as do the *segundas, terças, quartas e quintas pretas* (Black Mondays, Tuesdays, Wednesdays, and Thursdays),[56] along to so many other artistic occupations of public spaces. These spaces are reinvented as sites for the production and dissemination of Black aesthetic-cultural knowledges.

This performance of continuous and self-reinforcing transit through nomadic spatialities, whether through a literal or symbolic reterritorializing occupation of places and non-places, turns these locations into an expressive element of these scenic movements and wanderings. They propose, in the *urbis* (the urban context) their ideal of demos and *kratos*, with another potential organicity for the cities, now conceived through the gaze of those who inhabit or request them.

In these firefly poetics—as cultural sign-body—move scenic writings that draw inspiration from thematic and performative pillars of the rituals and cosmologies from religions of African origin, intricately woven by voice solfeggios and the moving body's circumscriptions and the poetics of its gestures, in the composition of fabulations, in references and identifications of metaphysical and philosophical cognitive systems, in the composite adherence of characters and themes to mythical and mystical figures of their diverse and vast narratology, as well as in the very exploration of the performative possibilities of dances, movements, and gestures of a wide ritual repertoire.

The performances by Grupo Nata, under the direction of Onisajé (Fernanda Júlia); alongside the ritualistic performance *Mulheres do àse*, by Edileusa Santos; the artistic creations of Rui Moreira; the productions by As Capulanas; the installation-performances by Zeca Ligiéro, inspired by Umbanda deities; and those by Grupo Caixa Preta; as so many others, remind us of the pioneering Teatro Experimental do Negro (Black Experimental Theater), the Balé Brasiliana, the Teatro Popular Solano Trindade, and, more recently, the stagings by João das Neves, who sought materials for exquisite plays in the cognitive and performative rituals and cosmological collections of Indigenous peoples and Black cultures, such as *A missa dos quilombos*, *A Santinha e os Congadeiros*, *Galanga*, *Chico rei!*, among many others.

Director Onisajé (Fernanda Júlia), reflecting on the use of this rich repertoire of metaphysical and teleological knowledges, shares:

> We don't work with the literal transposition of the liturgy onto the stage; rather, we focus on the composition of an element, a texture, a theme, an image to work with. This approach does not hinder our engagement with Brecht, Grotovisck, Cuti, Ângelo Fábio, Bando de Teatro Olodum, Os Crespos, and, indeed, with all contemporary theatrical theories. We're doing theater, we're not practicing religion. The decision to create a theater, to stage a play where the inspiration is drawn from Candomblé liturgy, allows us to bring the heritage and memory of our ancestors onto the stage. We shall blacken (a verb I steadfastly employ) the narrative, for we are creating, grounded in our impressions, our stances, and primarily, our view of the world.[57]

Along the same lines, while exploring other evocations, many productions draw inspiration from an imaginative Africa that excels in creating technologies and sciences throughout its history—a fact that is often overlooked, neglected, or obliterated. Several productions engage with techno-digital poetics, prevalent in Afrofuturism and hip-hop aesthetics, where the fusion of visual and sound samplings creates a striking sensory and perceptual explosion, as seen in productions by Grupo Legítima Defesa—particularly *Black Brecht: E se Brecht fosse negro?* (Black Brecht: What if Brecht was Black?)—as well as in the works by Capulanas and Narradores and in the plays by Aldri Anunciação.

The production of impressive visual and sound images marks this alliance between theater and technology, significantly influencing the conception and "dramaturgical structure (idealization and writing of the play), as well as the foundations of staging (conception and organization of the spectacular object) and, ultimately, the parameters of representation and performance (actors' work)," as Tonezzi states.[58]

Isaacsson adds that "scenic intermediality introduces a level of perceptual tension, either by blurring the boundaries between the real and the virtual through unconventional entanglement procedures, or by accentuating the inherent distinctions among various medias." Within these alliances between the arts and technologies, "intermediality emerges as a performative principle,"[59] a force that generates a compelling cognitive experience. Mediated by technoculture, this approach establishes a remarkable sensory and semantic appeal in the communication with the spectator.

In its realm, the image of the canvas-body is also a manifest mode of time, a time-body composed of ritornellos, recurrences, and threads, but also of becomings and scrutinies, a memory of the future that handwrites, engraves, translates, and transcreates Black experiences, forging new ways for the self to harmonize with the other. As Roubine points out, "theater is also movement and change, since representation is not only an inscription in a space, but the scansion of a duration."[60]

These aspects and fragments briefly pointed out here do not exhaust or reduce the multiplicity, diversity, polyphony, and singularity of these experiences nor the polyvalence of their ideals or even their aporias. Rather, they display the fruitful existence of these dramaturgical and scenic practices in the history of contemporary Brazilian theater. By aiming to disrupt the bias that denies Black people and their history in Brazilian theatrical and social traditions; by refusing the interdiction of their bodies by misshapen exclusionary forms, which are engendered by restrictive universalist ideals and tyrannical dual images enunciating a racist imagery; and by sculpting Black personhood, and everything that inhabits it, as a continent also capable of experiencing joy, pleasures, and affections, these groups and movements spread a strong effect of realness, presence, and belonging, and they make up an aesthetic tradition centered on Black and African elements and established as an erasure of the *doxa*, as a choreography of alterity, as Presence, a full-bodied presence that highlights the most polyphonic shades of Blackness on stages and in the streets.

Thus, this contemporary Black theater draws from an outstanding ethical function, expressing a set of values emanating from ancestral epistemologies, philosophies, and perceptions, from our *africanias*, from the oldest to the most contemporary ones. In their *afrografias*, in vocal twists, in the body's scores and spirals, they weave a powerful, thought-provoking, and libertarian *gesta*, which also appeals to the affective memory of all spectators. These *afrografias* resemanticize everyday life and affect individual and collective histories, aiming to expand the focus of our retinas and the gaps of our listening, revitalizing stages and, perhaps, expanding the core of our experiences, including aesthetic ones.

In this firefly poetics, one glimpses the persistent need to challenge the system. A system already constellated by flickering sparkles that flutter, emitting disturbing signals in the continuum of scenic lineages that now establish themselves as an erasure of the misspelled, as a potential choreography of diversity, as a presence capable of "*breaking through* the horizon of totalitarian constructions," as Didi-Huberman says, echoing Pasolini and Benjamin.[61] These totalitarian constructions bear witness to the power of marginalized cultures to disrupt repressive systems, and they "recognize the true capacity of historical, thus political, resistance, of their anthropological work of *survival*" of such cultures.[62] To ignore them would be "not to see the space—though it may be interstitial, intermittent, nomadic, improbably located—of openings, of possibilities, of flashes, *in spite of all*."[63] As Toni Morrison states: "All of us, readers and writers, are bereft when criticism remains too polite or too fearful to notice a disrupting darkness before its eyes."[64]

The canvas-body. A Black body. Black: a powerful, inventive, porous word. Black: an epistemic system, a wisdom, not merely skin, epidermis, a lamentation or regret. Black: "a minimal word territory—one syllable—on which Hope must land one day, big time. . . . Will it fit?" asks Camargo.[65]

A thin blade or a delicate gesture, Blackness, on its multiple faces, is performed in the movements of resurgent images, sometimes disturbing, rasping, screaming, thundering; sometimes tender, whispering, paused, and dotted; sometimes comical, sometimes dramatic; sometimes epiphanic and bright. Yet, always insistent, translucent, and yearning, like the insurgent lights of fireflies.

ON SPIRAL TIME, CONDENSATIONS

Man himself is an "object" [*ma*] in motion for he is an around-path-goer [*n'zungi a nzila*], in his upper and lower world. — BUNSEKI FU-KIAU, *African Cosmology of the Bantu-Kôngo*

As a call and response, time ebbs and flows in spirals, reinaugurating us in its kinesis. In the turns of time, we are. *Ntangu* time, sunlight time, time crossed in the wind, embodied experienced time. Time that echoes into other times, whether in the act of dissemination or the act of retreat. Time is also *tanga*, writing and dancing. To write is to inscribe in the dancing, vocalizing, singing, and drumming body, the time that constitutes spirals.

Throughout these compositions, we adorned ourselves in ancestralities. A powerful gnosis, ancestrality is installed and expanded through curves and ritornellos. A relational mater principle that interconnects everything that exists in the cosmos and covers it all in radiation and vital energy that ensures that each being, including the person and their surroundings, can have a concomitantly common and specific sort of existence, in the diversity of their nature. Channel of the vital force, the ancestral conception is like a ball of yarn; it includes, in the same phenomenological circuit, the deities, cosmic nature, fauna, flora, physical elements, the dead, the living, and those who are yet to be born,

FIGURE 6.1. Diego Alcantara, *Quaseilhas* (play). Photo: Taylla de Paula, 2018.

conceived as bonds of a necessary complementarity, in a continuous process of transformation and becoming. In its realm, everything establishes interdependent and mutually constitutive relationships.

Ancestrality is carved out by a curved, recurring, bonded time; a spiral time that circles back, restores, and transforms, impacting everything. An ontological time experienced as contiguous and simultaneous movements of retroaction, prospection, and reversibility, dilation, expansion and containment, contraction and relaxation, the synchronization of instances composed of present, past, and future. The curves of ancestrality are ruled by worshipped ancestors, whose immanence and presence are sine qua non conditions for the rhythmic and continuous flow of existence. Ancestors, repositories of accumulated life experiences, facilitate the transposition of intersecting *nzilas* and crossed crossings, and ensure the possibility of permanence of beings in their differentiated existences. Hence, ancestors are remembered and celebrated as sources of knowledge and rejuvenation.

Within the orbit of ancestral temporality, the precedence of movement nuances events, fostering a perpetual process of transformation. Birth, maturation, and death become natural contingencies, essential for the mutational and regenerative dynamics inherent in all vital and existential cycles. This cyclic movement engenders both permanence and repetition within difference. In this ceaseless process of "coming-and-going of life . . . there is no end," for "life is a continuum through many stages . . . in which there is no death or resurrection," for "life is a permanent process of change."[1] Or, as Padilha summarizes: "Death does not cut off communication with the living, since, due to the primacy of the vital force, all beings interact and, therefore, communicate. Everything is part of the same syntagmatic chain, without exclusion; the realms of the living and the dead interpenetrate each other, shaping a significant universe."[2] Even in death, in the dynamics of transformations, there is a prophetic gesture of becoming as a reminiscence of the metamorphosis that is necessary for the urgency, emergence, and continuity of life and the sacred breath that perennially underwrites/manifests itself in everything. Ancestors are born from death, and the rites of passage ensure their transcendence and permanence. Ancestors are an accumulation of knowledge that encompasses all existence in their surroundings, including nature, of which they are part and in which they are nourished.

In *Under the Frangipani*, by Mia Couto, a *xipoco*, a dead man who did not reach the dimension of remembered ancestor, cries out:

> For years, I was an esteemed inhabitant of life, a person of respectable origin. Though I was an upright citizen while alive, my death was inglorious. . . . As they didn't assign me a proper funeral, I became a ghost [*xipoco*], one of those souls who wander from somewhere to nowhere. Seeing as I hadn't been given a formal send-off, I ended up as a dead man who couldn't find his death. I shall never be elevated to the position of an ancestor [*xicuembo*], someone well and truly dead and gone for good, with a right to be invoked and cherished by the living. . . . I belong to the fellowship of those who are unremembered.[3]

To be remembered, reclaimed, and celebrated demands one to "re-die."[4] The prefix *re-* calls us to the need for a turn, for a do-over, a retrospection, a retroaction. Simultaneously, it also hints at a repetition to come, to be produced ahead, as a memory of the future. Returning—that is, becoming in/coming back to the past—is bonded to reconnecting, restoring, and reactivating the future through the prefix *re*.

Being remembered means participating, embodying a present presence within the interludes, courses, and interlines of life. It means landing on the spi-

FIGURE 6.2. Renata Vaz, *Aparecida* (play, Breve Cia). Photo: Fabrício Belmiro, 2019.

rals, as an *in-being* recorded and integrated into the dynamic circuit of memory and kinesis, as a quality of movement. It means underwriting multiple temporalities, as a floating being on simultaneous surfaces; embodying time within the Kalunga temporality, "an ocean of waves/radiations," composed of "biological, material, intellectual and spiritual treasures accumulated in scrolls [*ku mpèmba*], the past, i.e., the perpetual bank of the generating/driving forces of life."[5]

Ancestral time defies the constraints of progressive linearity, avoiding a relentless march toward an inexhaustible end and pathos. It does not conform to closed centripetal circles of repetitions of the same. In the spirals of ancestral time, everything moves back and forth, not as a mere specular similarity or a dominance of the same, but as an installation of knowledge, a *sophya*. This knowledge is not inert or paralyzing; instead, it kinesthetically remakes and accumulates itself in the indefinite sea-ocean of ancestral time—Kalunga time, Nzambi and Olorum time. It embodies a completeness in-itself, a gourd bowl filled with instances of continuous present, past, and future, with no elision or foreclosure, serenely enduring across an endless array of time. Spiral time.

In this ambience, to return is not to repeat the lived experience as the same or as sameness, because, as Ngũgĩ wa Thiong'o beautifully translates, in the African cosmoperception, "those of us who are in the present are all potential mothers and fathers of those who will follow. Reverencing the ancestors means to truly revere life, its continuity and change. We are the children of those who were here before us, but we are not their identical twins, just as we will not beget beings identical with ourselves.... In this way, the past becomes our source of inspiration; the present, a breathing arena; and the future our collective aspiration."[6]

Spiral time results from a complex entanglement of cosmic movements, encompassing both retrospective and prospective dimensions. This includes all beings and things, existing in their multiple forms and realms, all natural and transcendental phenomena, from the most intimate family relationships to broader and more diverse social and communal practices and expressions. It extends to materialities of the present, the epiphanies of the future, and even the emanations and resonances of the vital forces and energies pulsating in movement. This intricate interplay ensures the survival of all beings and the cosmos, in their completeness and wholeness.

Spiral time manifests itself through a prism of formulations and *africanias*, its canvas-bodies, forms that rule *oralituras*, means and modes of veridiction, as a force of the permanence and the Presence of ancestrality, pregnant with kinesis, curves, undulations, asymmetries, circumlocutions. Whether in healing medicinal practices, in the manufacturing of fabrics and utensils, in architectural forms, in the narrative and poetic voice textures, in music and sonorities, in sculpture and in the art of attires and masks, in bodily games, in African-inspired dances, in religious systems, in models of social organization, in modes of relationship between peoples and between the human and the divine, and, particularly, in the experience of spiral time, ancestrality pulsates and prevails, spreading, in radio-vibration waves, the vital force.

Within this thought and perspective, "Kalûnga, the principle-god-of change, is a force in motion, and because of that our earth and everything in it is in perpetual motion. Man himself is an 'object' [*ma*] in motion for he is an around-path-goer [*n'zûngi a nzila*], in his upper and lower world."[7] Thus:

Diâdi nza-Kôngo kandongila: Mono i kadi kia dingo-dingo (kwènda-vutukisa) kinzungidila ye didi dia ngolo zanzîngila. Ngiena, kadi yateka kala ye kalulula ye ngina vutuka kala ye kalulula.

Here is what the Kongolese Cosmology taught me: I am going-and-coming-back-being around the center of vital forces. I am because I was and re-was before, and that I will be and re-be again.[8]

At the crossroads of wisdoms that travel with the peoples across the diasporas, the memory of this knowledge was transported from the Africas to the Americas by embodied practices. In them, in their shared apparatus—speeches, songs, oral texts, languages, sound rhythms, danced gestures, choreographic movements, costumes, accessories, ceremonial objects, adornments, luminosities, skin inscriptions, spatialities, processions, celebrations—and in their philosophical and religious cosmoperception, textual, historical, sensory, organic, and conceptual repertoires of distant Africa, scores of African knowledge and wisdom, the alternate body of recreated identities, a patchwork of memories, reminiscences, and incomplete memory lapses, the grammar of shared affections—in short, the corpus of memory that carves out and crosses the torments that come from the crossings in the Ocean Sea and through every crossroad is all reorganized.

Imbued with polychromy by its various symbolic constitutive crossings, the body is a place of a knowledge that is continuously recreated and remitted, as well as of the constant transformations of the cultural corpus and the time that conceives and structures it. It is *nzila*, that is, path, a repertoire of thoughts that stylistically and ontologically graph this body/corpus as a locus and environment of wisdom and memory. These ideas and conceptions are also graphed in one of the most important kinds of African inscriptions, transcreated in multiple ways in African Brazilian religions: the cosmograms, scratched points, cartographies of these ontologies, signs of the cosmos and its derivations.

The body dances the time that is graphed and engraved in its movements. The body in performance restores, expresses, and simultaneously produces this knowledge, also graphed in the memory of gestures. Gestures, the poiesis of movement, sculpt and delineate undulating sonorities in the air, giving visual form to music and to the rhythmic complex of sonorities and vocalities, and creating "the external form of the poem in the space."[9] Thus, "a good dancer is one who converses with music, clearly hears and feels the beats, and is capable of using different parts of the body to create visualization of the rhythms."[10] Or, as Sodré also states, in Black culture "the interdependence between music and dance affects the formal structures of both, in such a way that music can be elaborated according to certain dance movements, just as dance can be conceived as a visual dimension of music."[11]

This marker of visuality composes what is graphed on the body, the inscriptions that constitute an image, a stylistic cultural sign. A hieroglyphic body.

Danced gestures. This is also how time is graphed, composed of body spinnings and the poetics of gestures that constitute and enact performance itself. Gestures are not only narrative or descriptive, but fundamentally performative.

In this danced aesthetic, spatial expansions mirror temporalities that curve in spinnings across the spaces; as the body twists over itself; in the movements of return and progress that bring about contraction and expansion in the earth and in the air; in the transverse swirls of counterclockwise rotation that precede and constitute the hours before and ahead, always a challenge, fraying ancestral presence in the present, always guided by the before, the during, and the after, simultaneously; in the circular geometries that include straight lines up, down, and sideways, entangling body movements and figuring the spiral shape of curved temporalities.

The choreographies of dance mimic this spiral circularity, whether expressed through the body's movement or in the spatial patterns that the spinning body draws around itself. The circumflex use of the torso, the shoulders folding and descending, the legs spinning and twisting, the ground-body, the movement of the feet touching and retouching the earth—the heart and pulse of the ancestors; and the soaring leap of the pole-body, connecting the human and the divine, all bear the imprints of memory. And as such, in an inclusive manner, they also beckon the bodily memory of all participants in the events across various realms, as they weave and rejuvenate themselves into the sacred breath of the divine, recreating the world of our ancestors and our own lived experiences. They re-semantizate our daily lives, expanding the cores of all beings, expanding the aesthetic, sensory, and epistemological experiences of our incomplete wisdoms, our doubts, our retinas, reanimating signs that once seemed deserted.

The subjects and the artistic forms that emerge from it all are made of memory, they make history.

The body is a gradience of sonorities, radiating in spiral waves. These sonorities emanate from vocalities, syllabic patterns, phrasings, and rhythmic phonemes, and from the repetition of speech and voice replicated by percussion instruments and all the musical ambience that, in temporal and temporizing ritornellos, spread cultural traits around. This underscores the significance, sophistication, and subtleties of rhythms: "In the technique of this musical form, the rhythm takes center stage (hence the importance of percussion instruments).... To sing/dance, to follow the rhythm, is akin to listening to the beats of one's own heart—it is feeling life while symbolically remembering death."[12]

Sounds vibrate in the choreography of the torso, in the palms of hands, in the movements of the feet, in the lines of the face. They lend voice to the language and its pronunciation, so the body echoes music, movement, voice, and dance, substantively and through a grammar of complementarity, in polyrhythms. In this ambience, the uttered word vibrates. Words, a dynamic force and principle, are best performed as synesthesia, a language that needs singing, dancing, rhythm, colors, performative gestures, smells, and flavors for its full realization and anticipatory oracular efficiency. Hence, the numinous nature and auratic power of the voice, through which the soloist repeats a theme, their vital force, and verses, sings, improvises on it, replicated by the choir, the cadence of call and response. In ancestral musicality, in which all sound is significant, the principles of return are rhythmically established and resonate in sound cyclic waves that progressively emanate and circumscribe people and their surroundings. In this musical weaving, the circumlocution, circulation, and sound, and instrumental emanation, stand out, and so does the indissociability between sonorities and all other semiotic systems that integrate and make up the performance. All sound/musical compositions, all the particularities of timbres and rhythms, are conceived as an indivisible unit, as they are mutually complementary. Singing invites dancing, which in turn embroiders musical sculptures in the air. The musical ambience can thus be read as a cosmogram, since it retains, in its spiral radiances and frequencies, the same qualities as these knowledge cartographies. Like a synthesis, it is a metonymy of the whole structure of Black ancestral thought; it is a cartography, a marker of consonance and movement. Sound rhythms, in themselves, as mise en abyme, reverberate culture in its integrity and the spiral time that structures them.

Through body performance, the selective memory of prior knowledge establishes and sustains itself in the social and cultural spheres. I called these gestures —these inscriptions and performative palimpsests, graphed by the body and its voices—*oralitura*.[13] The wisdoms of *oralitura* indicate the presence of a stylistic, mnemonic, culturally constituent feature, inscribed in the *graphya* of the moving body, in its imbued sounds and vocalities. Like a craft knife, this kinesthetic trace inscribes wisdoms, values, concepts, worldviews, and styles. Thus, every trace of memory, be it inscribed as written text, as voice, gesture, or body, is graphed in the constitution of subjects as repertoires of knowledge, as inscriptions, as alternate *graphyas* of knowledge. From this perspective, we can argue, after all, that there are no cultures without a writing system, since many peoples and societies inscribe, safeguard, nourish, and convey their knowledge repertoires in/through other memory environments, including their performance practices.

The dancing body produces, transfers, and transcreates wisdoms, within an aesthetic inaugurated by the ethics of a thought in which beauty is never disinterested or unnecessary, but holds the value of an asset, a good for the whole collectivity.

In the ethics of Black cultures, art is a good, an offering, and a gift.

The ancestors' gaze and voice ensure existence, as the memory of the ancestors guarantees the very production of memory. As long as our ancestors remember us, we will still be (here). In the sung-images, image-songs, dancing, body paintings and *graphyas*, they are the ones who still remember us and allow for our permanence here.

These *sophyas* and wisdoms testify that, just as there is no total, absolute, and complete reminiscence, oblivion also belongs to the order of incompleteness.

FIGURE 6.3. Leda Maria Martins, 2023. Photo: Rafael Mota. Archive of the author.

At these crossroads, in these circular trails, the gradiences and tuning forks of memory are fallen-off mementos of imperfect memory lapses, serving as bonds in the improvisation that embroiders African remains, residues, and traces in new expressive forms. In the dynamics of their temporalities, the most primal sense of the term *religion*—etymologically derived from the Latin word *religare*, meaning to reconnect, to restitute, to restore, to reattach—is performed. The reminiscences shine in the luminosity of vital forces, emanating the breath and the aromas of the sacred that inhabits us. Gestures are times that rhyme with feelings, as the poets teach us.

In the body, time dances. The body in performance is the place of what, curvilinearly, still and already is, of what could and can come to be, for existing in the simultaneity of presence and belonging. A has-already-been in the *yet to come*, in the *again to come*, and in the *being*.

A body, a time, a gesture of memory. The chords of ancestrality create supplements that cover the many hiatuses, gaps, and ruptures forged by abysmal diasporas, replacing something that seemed inexorably submerged in the crossings of paths, but is perennially transcreated, reincorporated, and restored by and in the cadences of its otherness, inscribed under the signs of reminiscence and presence in the curvilinear spirals of time. A knowledge, a wisdom.

List of Performances and Theatrical Works

Alguma coisa a ver com uma missão, directed by Os Crespos; written by Allan da Rosa and Os Crespos (Os Crespos, 2016)

A missa dos quilombos, directed by Luiz Fernando Lobo; written by João das Neves (Companhia Ensaio Aberto, 2002)

Antônia, directed by Sanara Rocha; written by Daniel Arcades (2016)

A Santinha e os Congadeiros, directed and written by João das Neves (2008)

Bombril, performance by Priscila Rezende (2010)

Buraquinhos, directed by Naruna Costa; written by Jhonny Salaberg (Carcaça de Poéticas Negras, 2019)

Cidade Vodu, directed and written by José Fernando Peixoto de Azevedo (Teatro de Narradores, 2016)

Como falar de coisas invisíveis, performance by Val Souza (2019)

De brasa e pólvora, directed by Os Crespos; written by Allan da Rosa (2016)

Galanga, Chico rei!, directed by João das Neves; written by Paulo César Pinheiro (2012)

Hamlet Sincrético, directed by Jessé Oliveira; written by Viviane Juguero (Caixa Preta, 2005)

Iyá Ilu, performance by Sanara Rocha (2017)

Mulheres do àse, directed and written by Edileusa Santos (2017)

Ninhos e revides: Mirando o Haiti, directed by Angelo Flávio; written by Os Crespos, Allan da Rosa, and Angelo Flávio (Os Crespos, 2016)

Outras rosas, written by Anderson Feliciano; performed by Soraya Martins (Coletivo Tropeço, 2017)

Preto, directed by Marcio Abreu; written by Marcio Abreu, Grace Passô, and Nadja Naira (Companhia Brasileiro de Teatro, 2017)

Pretoperitamar, O caminho que vai dar aqui, directed by Anelis Assumpção; written by Ana Maria Gonçalves and Grace Passô (2019)

Q'Eu Isse, directed by Rui Moreira; written by Adyr Assumpção (Cia. Será Que, 2008)

Quando Efé, directed by Leandro Belilo (Cia Fusion, 2014)

Quaseilhas, directed and written by Diego Araúja (2018)

Traga-me a cabeça de Lima Barreto, directed by Onisajé (Fernanda Júlia); written by Luiz Marfuz; performed by Hilton Cobra (2017)

Vaga Carne, directed, written, and performed by Grace Passô; creative team: Kenia Dias, Nadja Naira, Nina Bittencourt, and Ricardo Alves Jr. (2018)

Violento, directed by Alexandre de Sena; written by Alexandre de Sena and Preto Amparo; performed by Preto Amparo (2017)

Notes

RITORNELLOS

1. Ritornellos mean return, the recurrence of something. Very common in poetic constructions, they are the creation of sound patterns through the returning movements of sounds, forming circular poetic structures.

COMPOSITION I: THEOSOPHIES, TIMES, AND THEORIES

All translations of chants and/or citations are ours, unless stated otherwise. [Trans.]

1. In Portuguese: *No corpo o tempo bailarina*. Verse of a chant the author commonly sings during her lectures. [Trans.]

2. In the original, the author also uses the term *scripture* when referring to writing. [Trans.]

3. The author uses *grafia* as any kind of inscription, be it written or bodily inscribed. In Portuguese, this literally means "written representation of a word; writing; transcription." Its literal translation into English (writing or spelling) resulted in some losses of meaning. Therefore, we transcreated the term into *graphya*, which resonates with the Greek word *sophya*, recovering partially the broader and deeper sense of *grafia* as deployed by the author, that is, as wisdom. In the cases in which the related verb *grafar* appears, we used the verb *to graph*. [Trans.]

4. *Ancestralidade*, in Portuguese, is a philosophical concept in African diasporic and African traditions and scholarships. [Trans.]

5. See Hesiod, *"Theogony" and "Works and Days."*

6. Reis, *Tempo, história e evasão*, 12.

7. See Bergson, *Matter and Memory*.

8. Bergson, *Matter and Memory*, 13. See also Eliade, *O mito do eterno retorno, arquétipos e repetição*.

9. See Rovelli, *A ordem do tempo*.

10. Reis, *Tempo, história e evasão*, 13.

11. Bosi, "Sobre tempo e história," 25.

12. Bosi, "Sobre tempo e história," 20. See also Pomian, "Tempo/temporalidade."

13. See Bidima, *La Philosophie négro-africaine*; Biyogo, *Histoire de la Philosophie africaine*; Imbo, *Introduction to African Philosophy*; Mundimbe, *Invention of Africa*.

14. Ricoeur, "Introdução," 22.

15. See also Ricoeur, *Tempo e narrativa*; Ricoeur, *A memória, a história, o esquecimento*.

16. Ricoeur, "Introdução," 15–16.

17. Ricoeur, "Introdução," 18–19.

18. Ricoeur, "Introdução," 21–22.

19. Merleau-Ponty, "Phenomenology and the Sciences of Man," 95.

20. Ricoeur, "Introdução," 23, 25.

21. See also Pomian, "Tempo/temporalidade"; Bosi, "Sobre tempo e história"; Eliade, *O mito do eterno retorno, arquétipos e repetição*; Doctors, *Tempo dos tempos*; Novaes, *Tempo e história*; Ricoeur, *A memória, a história, o esquecimento*; Rovelli, *A ordem do tempo*.

22. Bosi, *O ser e o tempo da poesia*, 116–17.

23. Bosi, "Sobre tempo e história," 28.

24. Bosi, "Sobre tempo e história," 27.

25. Bosi, "Sobre tempo e história," 27.

26. *Oralitura* is a term coined by Leda Maria Martins to designate the stories and ancestral knowledge passed down not only through literature, but also in cultural performance manifestations—such as Congados. It is not equal to "oral literature," so we kept the term in Portuguese. [Trans.]

In the Anglophone world, *orature* or folk literature—a genre of literature that is spoken or sung as opposed to that which is written, could apply. According to Ngũgĩ wa Thiong'o, *orature* transcends both written and oral literature as it is based not on words, but on the fusion of many art forms in order to create a cohesive narrative experience. See also Ngũgĩ, "Notes Towards a Performance Theory of Orature." [Trans.]

27. Finnegan, *Where Is Language?*, 88–89.

28. Pomian, "Tempo/temporalidade," 137.

29. Hegel, *Philosophy of History*, 99.

30. Aguessy, "Traditional African Views and Apperceptions," 96.

31. Aguessy, "Traditional African Views and Apperceptions," 97.

32. Taylor, *Archive and Repertoire*, 18.

33. Roach, *Cities of the Dead*, 34.

34. Roach, *Cities of the Dead*, 45.

35. León-Portilla, *Los antiguos mexicanos a través de sus crónicas y cantares*, 39.

36. Toltec poem in León-Portilla, *Los antiguos mexicanos a través de sus crónicas y cantares*, 39.

37. A note on the subheading for this section: *Nzila* means "path" in Kimbundu, hence "*nzilas* cruzadas" could also be translated as "crossroads." We kept the term in Kimbundu to preserve the author's style. [Trans.]

38. Schechner, *Performance Theory*, 35.

39. Schechner, *Performance Theory*, 35.

40. Schechner, *Performance Theory*, 35.

41. Schechner, *Performance Theory*, 30.

42. Schechner, *Performance Theory*, 34.

43. Roach, *Cities of the Dead*, 26.

44. See Taylor, *Archive and Repertoire*; Roach, *Cities of the Dead*.

45. Taylor, *Archive and Repertoire*, 3.

46. Taylor, *Archive and Repertoire*, 2.

47. Taylor, *Archive and Repertoire*, 3.

48. Taylor, *Archive and Repertoire*, 15.

49. Zumthor, *Performance, recepção, leitura*, 35–36.

50. Connerton, *How Societies Remember*, 3.

51. Connerton, *How Societies Remember*.

52. Connerton, *How Societies Remember*, 35.

53. Connerton, *How Societies Remember*, 4–5.

54. Nora, "Between Memory and History: Les Lieux de Memoire," 284–300.

55. See Martins, *Afrografias da memória*; Martins, "Performances do tempo espiralar."

COMPOSITION II: THE CURVED TIMES OF MEMORY

1. Couto, *Under the Frangipani*, 43.

2. Jones, *Blues People*, 27–28.

3. An *Opele* is a divination chain used in traditional African and African American (in a broader sense) religions. [Trans.]

4. See Roach, "Culture and Performance in the Circum-Atlantic World," 61.

5. Tavares, *Gramáticas das corporeidades afrodiaspóricas*, 22.

6. Turner, *From Ritual to Theatre*, 82.

7. Aguessy, "Traditional African Views and Apperceptions," 84–85.

8. Aguessy, "Traditional African Views and Apperceptions," 93–94.

9. Aguessy, "Traditional African Views and Apperceptions," 101.

10. Santos, "Tradição e contemporaneidade," cited in Santos, *Corpo e ancestralidade*, 112.

11. See Martins, "A cena em sombras"; Martins, *A cena em sombras*; Martins, *Afrografias da memória*.

12. See Martins, "A cena em sombras"; Martins, *A cena em sombras*; Martins, *Afrografias da memória*; Fu-Kiau, "Ntanga-Tandu-Kola: The Bantu-Kongo Concept of Time"; Fu-Kiau, "A visão Bântu-Kôngo da sacralidade do mundo natural"; Thompson, *Flash of the Spirit*.

13. Santos, *Os Nagô e a morte*, 130–31.

14. Santos, *Os Nagô e a morte*, 165.

15. Gates, *Signifying Monkey*, 8–10.

16. Gates, *Signifying Monkey*, 6. See also Martins, *A cena em sombras*; Martins, *Afrografias da memória*.

17. Sodré, *Pensar nagô*, 187–88.

18. "The Congados, or Reinados, are an alternative religious system that has instituted itself in the very realm of the Catholic religion, in which the devotion to certain saints (Our Lady of the Rosary, Saint Benedict, Santa Iphigenia, and Our Lady of the Mercies) is accomplished by means of African-style performance rituals, with their metaphysi-

cal symbolic system, customs, choreography, organization, values, aesthetic conceptions, and particular worldview on which they are based." See Martins, "Performances of Spiral Time." [Trans.]

19. *Giras* refer to circle dances and modes of structuring spatial arrangements in Black cultural practices.

20. Fu-Kiau, "A visão Bântu-Kôngo da sacralidade do mundo natural," 8. This is a translation by Makota Valdina Pinto of a text by Fu-Kiau. In an interview with Tiganá Santana (in Santos, "A cosmologia africana dos Bantu-Kongo por Bunseki Fu-Kiau," 230–33), Pinto asserts having translated Fu-Kiau's manuscripts from French. She does not mention the exact source of the aforementioned translation into Brazilian Portuguese, but it contains some excerpts of Fu-Kiau's "Earth: The Mysterious 'Futu' to Life." Since she does not provided the exact source, the translation of Fu-Kiau's excerpts are ours and based on Pinto's translation. [Trans.]

21. Fu-Kiau, "A visão Bântu-Kôngo da sacralidade do mundo natural," 2.

22. Fu-Kiau, *Self-Healing Power and Therapy*, 111, quoted in Fu-Kiau, "A visão Bântu-Kôngo da sacralidade do mundo natural," 1.

23. Fu-Kiau, "A visão Bântu-Kôngo da sacralidade do mundo natural," 1–2.

24. Oliveira, *Cosmovisão africana no Brasil*, 68.

25. Fu-Kiau, *African Cosmology of the Bântu-Kôngo*, 42.

26. Fu-Kiau, *African Cosmology of the Bântu-Kôngo*, 54.

27. Cunha, "Ntu: Introdução ao pensamento filosófico Bantu," 26. See also Giroto, "O universo mágico-religioso negro africano e afro-brasileiro."

28. Oliveira, *Cosmovisão africana no Brasil*, 63.

29. *Terreiros* is a Candomblé term, meaning house of worship and its surroundings. [Trans.]

30. Aguessy, "Traditional African Views and Apperceptions," 86.

31. Leite, *A questão ancestral*, 35.

32. Leite, *A questão ancestral*, 35.

33. Oliveira, *Cosmovisão africana no Brasil*, 114.

34. Padilha, *Entre voz e letra*, 10.

35. Luz, *Cultura negra em tempos pós-modernos*, 90.

36. Luz, *Cultura negra em tempos pós-modernos*, 90.

37. Luz, *Cultura negra em tempos pós-modernos*, 90, quoting Sodré.

38. Oliveira, *Cosmovisão africana no Brasil*, 52.

39. Mbiti, *African Religion and Philosophy*, 21–22. In this regard, see also Soyinka, *Myth, Literature, and the African World*.

40. Roach, *Cities of the Dead*.

41. Leite, "Valores civilizatórios em sociedades negro-africanas," 44.

42. Braga, *Ancestralidade afro-brasileira*, 99.

43. Fu-Kiau, *African Cosmology of the Bântu-Kôngo*, 71.

44. A *ciranda* is a Brazilian folk dance similar to the ring-a-ring o' roses. [Trans.]

45. Oliveira, *Cosmovisão africana no Brasil*, 50.

46. Fu-Kiau, "A visão Bântu-Kôngo da sacralidade do mundo natural," 8.

47. Murray, *Omni-Americans*, 54.

48. *Africanias* refers to the reconstruction of African performance practices in new formats in Brazil.

49. Murray, *Hero and the Blues*, 88.

50. Thompson, *Flash of the Spirit*, 5.

51. Santana, "Tradução, interações, e cosmologias africanas," 73.

52. Cunha, "Ntu: Introdução ao pensamento filosófico Bantu," 26.

53. Thompson, *Flash of the Spirit*, 9.

54. Jones, *Blues Peoples*, 28–29.

55. Cunha, "Ntu: Introdução ao pensamento filosófico Bantu," 26.

56. Santos, "Tradição e contemporaneidade," cited in Santos, *Corpo e ancestralidade*, 120.

57. Fu-Kiau, *African Cosmology of the Bântu-Kôngo*, 97.

COMPOSITION III: POETICS OF *ORALITURA*

1. *Gesta*, as in *canções de gesta*, in Portuguese; *chanson de geste*. [Trans.]

2. Bosi, *O ser e o tempo da poesia*, 13.

3. Bosi, *O ser e o tempo da poesia*.

4. Bosi, *O ser e o tempo da poesia*, 40.

5. Bosi, *O ser e o tempo da poesia*, 42.

6. Samain, "As imagens não são bolas de sinuca. Como pensam as imagens," 22.

7. Samain, "As imagens não são bolas de sinuca. Como pensam as imagens," 22–23.

8. In Portuguese: *No tempo o corpo bailarina*. Verse of a chant the author commonly sings during her lectures. [Trans.]

9. See Thompson, *African Art in Motion*, XII.

10. Fu-Kiau, "A Powerful Trio: Drumming-Singing-Dancing," quoted in Malone, *Steppin' on the Blues*, 9.

11. Fu-Kiau, "A Powerful Trio: Drumming-Singing-Dancing," quoted in Malone, *Steppin' on the Blues*, 11.

12. Fu-Kiau, "Ntanga-Tandu-Kola: The Bantu-Kongo Concept of Time," 21.

13. I use *afrografias* to refer to knowledge(s) inscribed and graphed by African-referenced embodied practices.

14. Rodrigues, *Bailarino-pesquisador-intérprete*, 96.

15. Rodrigues, *Bailarino-pesquisador-intérprete*, 43–44.

16. *Rebolejo* means twerking. [Trans.]

17. *Ginga* is moving the body in a specific way; it might refer to attack-and-defense movements in capoeira; swinging; swag. [Trans.]

18. Sodré, *Samba, o dono do corpo*, 11.

19. Silva, *O corpo na capoeira*, 57–60.

20. Ligiéro, *Corpo a corpo*, 129.

21. Zumthor, *Introdução à poesia oral*, 207.

22. Galard, *A beleza do gesto*, 27.

23. Galard, *A beleza do gesto*, 35.

24. Galard, *A beleza do gesto*, 25.

25. Galard, *A beleza do gesto*, 37.

26. Zumthor, *Introdução à poesia oral*, 207, 209.

27. Malone, *Steppin' on the Blues*, 15.

28. Malone, *Steppin' on the Blues*, 11.

29. Sodré, *Samba, o dono do corpo*, 22.

30. Rodrigues, *Bailarino-pesquisador-intérprete*, 53–54.

31. A *filha-de-santo* is an initiate of Candomblé. [Trans.]

32. Martins, *A dança de Yemanjá Ogunté sob a perspectiva estética do corpo*, 139–40.

33. Cunha, "Ntu: Introdução ao pensamento filosófico Bantu," 35.

34. *Corpografia* in Portuguese. [Trans.]

35. Santos, *Os Nagô e a morte*, 48–49.

36. Sodré, *Samba, o dono do corpo*, 19.

37. Sodré, *Samba, o dono do corpo*, 21.

38. Jones, *Blues People*, 26.

39. Sodré, *Samba, o dono do corpo*, 19–20.

40. Zumthor, *Introdução à poesia oral*, 177.

41. Zumthor, *Introdução à poesia oral*, 66.

42. Zumthor, *A letra e a voz*, 244.

43. Martins, *Afrografias da memória*.

44. Santos, *Os Nagô e a morte*, 46.

45. Amaral, *Matimo, Masaho ni dzitekatekane nya vatonga*, 44, quoted in Santos, "A cosmologia africana dos Bantu-Kongo por Bunseki Fu-Kiau," 171.

46. Zumthor, *Introdução à poesia oral*, 279.

47. Padilha, *Entre voz e letra*, 16.

48. Sodré, *A verdade seduzida*, 176. See also Martins, *Afrografias da memória*.

49. Sodré, *Samba, o dono do corpo*, 20.

50. Jones, *Blues People*, 18.

51. Malone, *Steppin' on the Blues*, 9.

52. Bebey, *African Music*, 122.

53. Jones, *Blues People*, 28.

54. *Vissungo* refers to responsorial music sung by enslaved Africans, not only while diamond and gold mining in the state of Minas Gerais. There were *vissungos* for the dawn, for the mealtime, for moments of joy, for burials, among other daily activities. *Ladainha* means litany. *Inguiziras* and *quizumbas* both mean predicament; confusion. *Corridinhos* are a type of dance. [Trans.]

55. Padilha, *Entre voz e letra*, 15.

56. *Embaixadas* are a part of Congado's celebrations. [Trans.]

57. Lucas, *Os sons do Rosário*, 75.

58. Lucas, *Os sons do Rosário*, 80.

59. Risério, *Oriki Orixá*, 35.

60. Risério, *Oriki Orixá*, 36.

61. Santos, "A cosmologia africana dos Bantu-Kongo por Bunseki Fu-Kiau," 71.

62. Fu-Kiau, *African Cosmology of the Bântu-Kôngo*, 93–95.

63. Yeda Pessoa de Castro, one of Brazil's greatest specialists in African languages, concludes that "historically, concerning African languages, those of the Bantu group were

the most important in the process of configuration of Brazilian Portuguese's profile, due to the antiquity and numerical superiority of its speakers and to the greatness of the dimension reached by its human distribution in colonial Brazil." Castro, *Falares africanos na Bahia*, 74–75. See also Queiroz, *Pé preto no barro branco*; Lopes, *Bantos, malês e identidade negra*; Vogt and Fry, *Cafundó, a África no Brasil*; Valdina O. Pinto's interview quoted in Santos, "A cosmologia africana dos Bantu-Kongo por Bunseki Fu-Kiau," 230–33.

64. See Martins, *A cena em sombras*.

65. Jones, *Blues People*, 28.

66. See Connerton, *How Societies Remember*, 33–34.

67. Maultsby, "Africanism in African-American Music," 189.

68. Connerton, *How Societies Remember*, 11–12.

69. Martins, *A dança de Yemanjá Ogunté sob a perspectiva estética do corpo*, 101; see Thompson, *Flash of the Spirit*.

70. Santos and Santos, *African Sacred Arts and Rituals in Brazil*, quoted in Santos, *Corpo e ancestralidade*, 38.

71. *Quilombolas* are *maroons*. [Trans.]

72. See Roberts and Roberts, "Body Memory," 86.

73. *Kizomba* designates a dance and musical genre originated in Angola around 1984. *Kizomba* means "party" in the Bantu language Kimbundu. [Trans.]

74. Oliveira, *Cosmovisão africana no Brasil*, 69.

75. Cunha, "Ntu: Introdução ao pensamento filosófico Bantu," 27.

76. Fu-Kiau, "A visão Bântu-Kôngo da sacralidade do mundo natural," 2.

77. Fu-Kiau, *African Cosmology of the Bântu-Kôngo*, 11.

COMPOSITION IV: MY DESTINY IS TO SING,
THE MYTHOPOETIC *GESTA* OF THE REINADOS

1. Soyinka, "Theatre in African Traditional Cultures," 342.

2. Roach, *Cities of the Dead*, 2.

3. In the corresponding *congadeiros* lexicon, the terms *guarda* or *terno* designate a specific group of dancers with their clothing, liturgical functions, and specific characteristics. [Trans.]

4. Turner, *From Ritual to Theatre*.

5. Variations of this account, as well as a more detailed study of the Congados, can be found in my book *Afrografias da memória*. See also Gomes and Pereira, *Negras raízes mineiras*; Lucas, *Os sons do Rosário*.

6. Dona Alzira Germana Martins, then sixty-five years old, Queen of Nossa Senhora das Mercês (Our Lady of Mercy) of the Irmandade de Nossa Senhora do Rosário do Jatobá (Fraternity of Our Lady of the Rosary of Jatobá). Interviews recorded on July 5, 1992, and April 3, 1996. The full song, in Brazilian Portuguese: "*Ô, vem Mariá / já com Deus / vem Mariá / Olê, vamo devagá / olê, vamo devagá / Moçambique não pode corrê / Moçambique não pode corrê / olê, vamo devagá.*" [Trans.]

7. "In Latin America, vows to saints are known as *mandas* or *promesas*. Traditionally, scholars of Latin American religion have understood this as 'propitiation' or a reciprocal

agreement made between a devotee and the saint figure chosen to fulfill a specific concern. Devotees to Roman Catholic saints will make a petition to a saint, asking for favors ranging from healing illnesses to completing journeys safely; in turn, when the petition is realized, the devotee will fulfill the contract made with the saint (Gruzinski 1995)." Vargas, *Encyclopedia of Latin American Religions*. [Trans.]

8. See "A Body of Adornments, Luminosities, and Polychromy," in this book.

9. See Roberts and Roberts, "Body Memory," 86.

10. Roach, "Culture and Performance in the Circum-Atlantic World," 61.

11. *Undamba*: from *Kimbanda*, meaning "healer," "shaman," in Kimbundu. See Oliveira, *Palavra Africana em Minas Gerais*. [Trans.]

12. On similar processes of resignification of Catholic sacraments in the Americas, see also Sklar, *Dancing with the Virgin*, 2001.

13. A note on the subheading for this section: *No corpo o tempo bailarina*, in Portuguese. This is part of a chant the author sings in her lectures. [Trans.]

14. Santos, *Os Nagô e a morte*, 49.

15. Thompson, *African Art in Motion*, XII.

16. Sodré, *Samba, o dono do corpo*, 67.

17. Sodré, *Samba, o dono do corpo*, 23, 68.

18. Roach, *Culture and Performance in the Circum-Atlantic World*, 125.

19. Roberts and Roberts, "Body Memory," 86.

20. Turner, *From Ritual to Theatre*, 82.

21. Fu-Kiau, "Ntanga-Tandu-Kola: The Bantu-Kongo Concept of Time," 33.

22. Carvalho, *Hábito da terra*.

23. Pereira, *Casa da palavra*, 143.

COMPOSITION V: A CANVAS-BODY, A FIREFLY POETICS

1. See Duarte, *Literatura e afrodescendência no Brasil*.

2. Silva, "Apresentação," 17.

3. Sérgio, "A cena mineira: Memória, identidade e protagonismo em BH," 38.

4. Silva, "Apresentação," 17.

5. Eugênio Lima's interview is quoted in Souza, "Reflexões sobre o teatro negro," 67–68.

6. Anunciação, *Trilogia do confinamento*, 120.

7. Anunciação, *Trilogia do confinamento*, 122–23.

8. Martin, *Theatre of the Real*, 176.

9. Martin, *Theatre of the Real*, 59.

10. Martin, *Theatre of the Real*, 176.

11. See the play's press release, Portal Geledés, "'Alguma coisa a ver com uma missão,' da Cia."

12. See the concept of *biographeme*. Barthes, *Camera Lucida*.

13. Zumthor, *Introdução à poesia oral*, 216–17.

14. Samain, "As imagens não são bolas de sinuca. Como pensam as imagens," 21–36.

15. Samain, "As imagens não são bolas de sinuca. Como pensam as imagens," 22, 23.

16. See Pereira and Gomes, *Ardis da imagem*.

17. Assis, "Pai contra mãe."

18. Samain, "As imagens não são bolas de sinuca. Como pensam as imagens," 33.

19. Martin, *Theatre of the Real*, 176.

20. *Aquilombamento* is a *quilombo*-like grouping; marronage. [Trans.]

21. Passô, "O teatro é uma espécie de aquilombamento."

22. Passô, "A produção negra é um farol para a arte brasileira."

23. Saturnino, "Ligeiro deslocamento do real," 98.

24. Fischer-Lichte, "Reality and fiction in contemporary theatre," 88.

25. Saturnino, "Ligeiro deslocamento do real," 102.

26. Boal, *Teatro do oprimido e outras poéticas políticas*.

27. Anunciação, *Trilogia do confinamento*, 119.

28. See Deleuze and Guattari, "How Do You Make Yourself a Body Without Organs?"

29. Paixão, "Por uma Sociologia do teatro negro feminino das Capulanas," 59.

30. Sérgio, "A cena mineira: Memória, identidade e protagonismo em BH," 39.

31. See Martins, "O feminino corpo da negrura," 111–21.

32. Alves, Uma entrevista [An interview], 971.

33. The performance *Como falar de coisas invisíveis* took place in São Paulo, March 18, 2019.

34. *Pelourinhos* means pillories. [Trans.]

35. *Quebrantos* means jinx, enchantment, evil eye. [Trans.]

36. Carlos, "Manifesta cabocla," 15–19.

37. Lorde, *Sister Outsider*, 40.

38. Ribeiro, "Quem somos: Mulheres negras no plural, nossa existência é pedagógica," 273.

39. Passô, "A produção negra é um farol para a arte brasileira."

40. Pimentel, "O Corpo como instrumento da arte: Conheça a performer Val Souza."

41. Lucinda, "Aviso da lua que menstrua," 91.

42. Collins, *Black Feminist Thought*, 113–14.

43. "*Eu-nós*" in the original. [Trans.]

44. Guimarães, "Constatação," 96.

45. In Portuguese: *aparecer* and *parecer*. [Trans.]

46. Bosi, *O ser e o tempo da poesia*, 14.

47. Zumthor, *Introdução à poesia oral*, 32.

48. Zumthor, *Introdução à poesia oral*, 216, 217.

49. Galard, *A beleza do gesto*, 27.

50. Zumthor, *Introdução à poesia oral*, 207.

51. Oliveira and Lopes, *Hamlet sincrético*, 9.

52. Villas Bôas, "Cidade Vodu," 24, 25.

53. Cerqueira, "O limite poroso entre o político e o estético na tragédia negra *Antônia*," 84.

54. See Portal Geledés, "'Alguma coisa a ver com uma missão,' da Cia."

55. See Glissant, *Introduction to a Poetics of Diversity*.

56. Reference to a series of events and encounters spread in Brazil that create Black conviviality territories, such as segundaPRETA (Black Monday), in Belo Horizonte, Minas Gerais, "Terça Afro" (Afro Tuesday), in São Paulo, and others. [Trans.]

57. Júlia Onisajé, "Entrevista," 19.

58. Tonezzi and Schulte, "Cena, tecnologia e inovação: Desafios para a formação da pesquisa em artes e espetáculo," 55.

59. Isaacsson, "Cruzamentos históricos: Teatro e tecnologia de imagem," 20, 22.

60. Roubine, *Introdução às grandes teorias do teatro*, 162.

61. Didi-Huberman, *Survival of the Fireflies*, 62–63.

62. Didi-Huberman, *Survival of the Fireflies*, 13.

63. Didi-Huberman, *Survival of the Fireflies*, 18.

64. Morrison, *Playing in the Dark*, 91.

65. Camargo, *O negro escrito*, 110–11.

NTANGU: ON SPIRAL TIME, CONDENSATIONS

1. Rui, *Eu e o outro*, 56.

2. Padilha, *Entre voz e letra*, 39.

3. Couto, *Under the Frangipani*, 1–2.

4. Couto, *Under the Frangipani*, 13.

5. Fu-Kiau, *African Cosmology of the Bantu–Kôngo*, 71.

6. Ngũgĩ, *Writers in Politics*, 139.

7. Fu-Kiau, *African Cosmology of the Bantu–Kôngo*, 22.

8. Fu-Kiau, *African Cosmology of the Bantu–Kôngo*, 5.

9. Zumthor, *Introdução à poesia oral*, 216–17.

10. Malone, *Steppin' on the Blues*, 15.

11. Sodré, *Samba, o dono do corpo*, 22.

12. Sodré, *Samba, o dono do corpo*, 23.

13. See Martins, *Afrografias da memória*, 21.

Bibliography

Adjaye, Joseph, ed. *Time in the Black Experience*. Greenwood Press, 1994.

Aguessy, Honorat. "Traditional African Views and Apperceptions." In *Introduction to African Culture: General Aspects*, edited by Alpha I. Sow, Ola Balogun, Honorat Aguessy, and Path Diagne. UNESCO, 1979. https://unesdoc.unesco.org/ark:/48223/pf0000037498.

Alves, Miriam. Uma entrevista [An interview]. In "African Brazilian Literature," edited by Leda Maria Martins, Carolyn Durham, Phyllis Peres, and C. Howell, special issue, *Callaloo* 18, no. 4 (1995): 970–72.

Amaral, Bernardo. *Matimo, Masaho ni dzitekatekane nya vatonga*. Apud, 2009.

Anunciação, Aldri. *Trilogia do confinamento*. Editora Perspectiva, 2020.

Assis, Machado de. "Pai contra mãe." In *Obras completas: Conto e teatro*, vol. 2. Editora Nova Aguilar, 1997.

Barthes, Roland. *Camera Lucida: Reflections on Photography*. Translated by Richard Howard. Hill and Wang, 1981.

Bebey, Francis. *African Music: A People's Art*. Translated by Josephine Bennett. Lawrence Hill, 1975.

Benveniste, Émile. *Problemas de linguística geral*. Vol. 2. Translated by Eduardo Guimarães et al. Pontes, 1989.

Bergson, Henri. *Matter and Memory*. Translated by Nancy Margaret Paul and W. Scott Palmer. Zone Books, 1988.

Bidima, J.-G. *La Philosophie négro-africaine*. Presses Universitaires de France, 1995.

Biyogo, G. *Histoire de la Philosophie africane: Le berceau egypcien de la Philosophie*. Vol. 1. L'Harmattan, 2006.

Boal, Augusto. *Teatro do oprimido e outras poéticas políticas*. 2nd ed. Civilização Brasileira, 1977.

Bosi, Alfredo. *O ser e o tempo da poesia*. Cultrix, 1990.

Bosi, Alfredo. "Sobre tempo e história." In *Tempo e história*, edited by Adauto Novaes. Companhia das Letras, 1992.

Braga, Júlio. *Ancestralidade afro-brasileira: O culto de Baba Egun*. Ceao-Ianamá, 1992.

Branco, Lucia Castello. "Escrever a loucura." Paper presented at V Congresso ABRALIC, Rio de Janeiro, UFRJ, July 31–August 3, 1996.

Camargo, Oswaldo de. *O negro escrito: Apontamentos sobre a presença do negro na literatura brasileira*. Secretaria de Estado da Cultura, 1987.

Campos, Haroldo de. "A linguagem do Iauaretê." In *Metalinguagem & outras metas, ensaios de teoria e crítica literária*, 4th ed. Perspectiva, 1992.

Carlos, Dione. *Dramaturgias do front*. Editora Primata, 2017.

Carlos, Dione. "Manifesta cabocla." In *Janela de dramaturgia, edição manifesto*, edited by Vinicius Souza. PBH/SMC, Instituto Unimed-BH, 2019.

Carvalho, Ruy Duarte de. *Hábito da terra: Poesia*. União dos Escritores Angolanos, 1988.

Castro, Yeda Pessoa de. *Falares africanos na Bahia: Um vocabulário afro-brasileiro*. Topbooks, 2001.

Cerqueira, Gustavo Melo. "O limite poroso entre o político e o estético na tragédia negra *Antônia*." *Legítima Defesa, uma Revista de Teatro Negro* 2, no. 2 (2016): 83–89.

Collins, Patricia Hill. *Black Feminist Thought: Knowledge, Consciousness, and the Politics of Empowerment*. Routledge, 2000.

Connerton, Paul. *How Societies Remember*. Cambridge University Press, 1989.

Couto, Mia. *Under the Frangipani*. Translated by David Brookshaw. David Philip, 2001.

Cunha, Henrique, Jr. "Ntu: Introdução ao pensamento filosófico Bantu." *Revista Educação em Debate* año 32, vol. 1, no. 59 (2010): 25–40.

Deleuze, Gilles, and Félix Guattari. "How Do You Make Yourself a Body Without Organs?" In *A Thousand Plateaus: Capitalism and Schizophrenia*, translated and with a foreword by Brian Massumi. University of Minnesota Press, 1987.

Didi-Huberman, Georges. *Survival of the Fireflies*. Translated by Lia Swope Mitchell. University of Minnesota Press, 2018.

Doctors, Marcio, ed. *Tempo dos tempos*. Jorge Zahar Editor, 2003.

Drewal, Margaret Thompson. *Yoruba Ritual: Performers, Play, Agency*. Indiana University Press, 1992.

Duarte, Eduardo de Assis, ed. *Literatura e afrodescendência no Brasil: Antologia crítica*. Editora UFMG, 2011.

Eliade, Mircea. *O mito do eterno retorno, arquétipos e repetição*. Translated by Manuela Torres. Editora Martins Fontes, 1981.

Finnegan, Ruth. *Where Is Language? An Anthropologist's Questions on Language, Literature and Performance*. Bloomsbury, 2015.

Fischer-Lichte, Erika. "Reality and Fiction in Contemporary Theatre." *Theatre Research International* 33, no. 1 (2008): 84–96.

Fu-Kiau, K. K. Bunseki. *African Cosmology of the Bântu-Kôngo: Principles of Life and Living*. Athelia Henrietta, 2001.

Fu-Kiau, K. K. Bunseki. "A visão Bântu-Kôngo da sacralidade do mundo natural." Translated by Makota Valdina Pinto. ACBANTU, 2015. https://estahorareall.wordpress.com /wp-content/uploads/2015/07/dr-bunseki-fu-kiau-a-visc3a30-bantu-kongo-da -sacralidade-do-mundo-natural.pdf.

Fu-Kiau, K. K. Bunseki. "Earth: The Mysterious 'Futu' to Life." In *Self-Healing Power and Therapy: Old Teachings from Africa*. Imprint Editions, [1991] 2003.

Fu-Kiau, K. K. Bunseki. "Ntangu-Tandu-Kolo: The Bantu-Kongo Concept of Time." In *Time in the Black Experience*, edited by Joseph K. Adjaye. Greenwood Press, 1994.

Galard, Jean. *A beleza do gesto*. Edusp, 1997.

Gates, Henry Louis, Jr. *The Signifying Monkey: A Theory of African American Literary Criticism*. Oxford University Press, 1988.

Giroto, Ismael. "O universo mágico-religioso negro africano e afro-brasileiro: Bantu e Nàgó." PhD diss., Universidade de São Paulo, 1999.

Glissant, Édouard. *Introduction to a Poetics of Diversity*. Translated by Celia Britton. Liverpool University Press, 2000.

Gomes, Núbia Pereira de Magalhães, and Edimilson de Almeida Pereira. *Negras raízes mineiras: Os Arturos*. EDUFJF/MinC, 1988.

Gonçalves, Ana Maria. *Um defeito de cor*. Editora Record, 2006.

Guimarães, Geni. "Constatação." In *Finally Us*, edited by Miriam Alves and Carolyn Durham. Three Continental, 1995.

Hegel, G. W. F. *The Philosophy of History*. Dover, 1956.

Hesiod. *"Theogony" and "Works and Days."* Translated by M. L. West. Oxford University Press, 1988.

Holloway, Joseph E., ed. *Africanisms in American Culture*. Indiana University Press, 1990.

Huyssen, Andreas. "Present Pasts: Media, Politics, Amnesia." *Public Culture* 12, no. 1 (2000): 21–38.

Imbo, Samuel Oluoch. *An Introduction to African Philosophy*. Rowman and Littlefield, 1998.

Isaacsson, Marta. "Cruzamentos históricos: Teatro e tecnologia de imagem." *ArtCultura* 13, no. 23 (2011): 7–22.

Jones, LeRoi. *Blues People: Negro Music in White America*. William Morrow and Company, 1963.

Júlia Onisajé, Fernanda. "Entrevista" [Interview]. *Legítima Defesa, uma Revista de Teatro Negro* 2, no. 2 (2016): 19.

Kagame, Alexis. *La Philosofie Bantu Comparée*. Présence Africaine, 1976.

Leite, Fábio. *A questão ancestral: África negra*. Casa das Áfricas; Palas Athena, 2009.

Leite, Fábio. "Valores civilizatórios em sociedades negro-africanas." In *Introdução aos estudos sobre África contemporânea*. Centro de Estudos Africanos da USP, 1984.

León-Portilla, Miguel. *Los antiguos mexicanos através de sus crónicas y cantares*, 5th ed. Fondo de Cultura Económica, 1977.

Lhansol, Maria Gabriela. *Lisboaleipsig I: O encontro do diverso*. Rolim, 1994.

Ligiéro, Zeca. *Corpo a corpo: Estudo das performances brasileiras*. Garamond, 2011.

Lopes, Nei. *Bantos, malês e identidade negra*. Forense Universitária, 1988.

Lorde, Audre. *Sister Outsider*. Crossing, 1984.

Lucas, Glaura. *Os sons do Rosário: O congado mineiro dos Arturos e Jatobá*. Editora UFMG, 2002.

Lucinda, Elisa. "Aviso da lua que menstrua." In *O semelhante*. Record, 2000.

Luz, Marco Aurélio. *Cultura negra em tempos pós-modernos*. 3rd ed. EDUFBA, 2008.

Malone, Jacqui. *Steppin' on the Blues: The Visible Rhythms of African American Dance*. University of Illinois Press, 1996.

Martin, Carol. *Theatre of the Real*. Palgrave Macmillan, 2013.

Martins, Leda Maria. *A cena em sombras*. Perspectiva, 1995.

Martins, Leda Maria. "A cena em sombras: Expressões do teatro negro no Brasil e nos Estados Unidos." PhD diss., Universidade Federal de Minas Gerais, 1991.

Martins, Leda Maria. *Afrografias da memória: O Reinado do Rosário no Jatobá*. Ed. Perspectiva; Mazza Edições, 1997.

Martins, Leda Maria. "A oralitura da memória." In *Brasil afro-brasileiro*, edited by Maria Nazareth Soares Fonseca. Autêntica, 2000.

Martins, Leda Maria. "O feminino corpo da negrura." *Revista de Estudos de Literatura* 4 (1996): 111–21. http://www.periodicos.letras.ufmg.br/index.php/aletria/article/view /1137>.

Martins, Leda Maria. "Performance del tiempo: Los Congados." *Conjunto, Revista de Teatro Latinoamericano* (2004): 3–14.

Martins, Leda Maria. "Performances do tempo espiralar." In *Performances, exílios, fronteiras: Errâncias territoriais e textuais*, edited by Graciela Ravetti and Márcia Arbex. FALE; UFMG; Pós-Lit, 2002.

Martins, Leda Maria. "Performances of Spiral Time." In *Performing Religion in the Americas: Media, Politics and Devotional Practices of the Twenty-First Century*, edited by Alyshua Galvez. Seagull Books, 2007.

Martins, Suzana. *A dança de Yemanjá Ogunté sob a perspectiva estética do corpo*. EGBA, 2008.

Matos, Claudia Neiva de, Elizabeth Travassos, and Fernanda Teixeira de Medeiros, eds. *Palavra cantada: Ensaios sobre poesia, música e voz*. 7 Letras, 2008.

Maultsby, Portia K. "Africanism in African-American Music." In *Africanisms in American Culture*, edited by Joseph E. Holloway. Indiana University Press, 1990.

Mbiti, John S. *African Religion and Philosophy*. 2nd ed. Heinemann Educational, 1999.

Merleau-Ponty, Maurice. "Phenomenology and the Sciences of Man." In *The Primacy of Perception: And Other Essays on Phenomenological Psychology, the Philosophy of Art, History, and Politics*, edited by William Cobb and James M. Edie. Northwestern University Press, 1964.

Morrison, Toni. *Playing in the Dark: Whiteness and the Literary Imagination*. Harvard University Press, 1992.

Mundimbe, V. Y. *The Invention of Africa: Gnosis, Philosophy, and the Order of Knowledge*. Indiana University Press; James Currey, 1988.

Murray, Albert. *The Hero and the Blues*. Vintage Books, 1995.

Murray, Albert. *The Omni-Americans: Black Experience and American Culture*. Vintage Books, 1983.

Ngũgĩ wa Thiong'o. *Decolonizing the Mind: The Politics of Language in African Literature*. James Currey; East African Educational Publishers, [1986] 2006.

Ngũgĩ wa Thiong'o. "Notes Towards a Performance Theory of Orature." *Performance Research* 12, no. 3 (2007): 4–7. https://doi.org/10.1080/13528160701771253.

Ngũgĩ wa Thiong'o. *Writers in Politics: A Re-Engagement with Issues of Literature and Society*. Revised and enlarged ed. James Currey; East African Educational Publishers, 1997.

Nora, Pierre. "Between Memory and History: Les Lieux de Memoire." In *History and Memory in African-American Culture*, edited by Geneviere Fabre and Robert O'Meally. Oxford University Press, 1994.

Novaes, Adauto, ed. *Tempo e história*. Companhia das Letras, 1992.

Oliveira, Amanda Sônia López de. *Palavra Africana em Minas Gerais*. FALE; UFMG, 2009.

Oliveira, Eduardo. *Cosmovisão africana no Brasil: Elementos para uma filosofia afrodescendente*, 2nd ed. Editora Gráfica Popular, 2006.

Oliveira, Jessé, and Vera Lopes, eds. *Hamlet sincrético, em busca de um teatro negro*. Caixa Preta, 2019.

O'Meally, Robert G., ed. *The Jazz Cadence of American Culture*. Columbia University Press, 1998.

Padilha, Laura Cavalcante. *Entre voz e letra: O lugar da ancestralidade na ficção angolana do século XX*. Eduff, 1995.

Paixão, Adriana. "Por uma Sociologia do teatro negro feminino das Capulanas: Indícios e percursos." In *Negras insurgências: Teatros e dramaturgias negras em São Paulo; perspectivas históricas, teóricas e práticas*, edited by Salloma Salomão Jovino da Silva. Capulanas Cia. de Arte Negra, 2018.

Passô, Grace. "A produção negra é um farol para a arte brasileira." Interview by Luisa Pecora. *Mulher no cinema*, January 21, 2019. https://mulhernocinema.com/entrevistas /grace-passo-a-producao-negra-e-um-farol-para-a-arte-brasileira.

Passô, Grace. "O teatro é uma espécie de aquilombamento." Interview by Mariana Filgueiras. *Revista Continente*, April 24, 2018. https://revistacontinente.com.br/secoes /entrevista/ro-teatro-e-uma-especie-de-aquilombamentor.

Pereira, Edimilson de Almeida. *Casa da palavra: Obra poética 3*. Mazza Edições, [1996] 2003.

Pereira, Edimilson de Almeida. "Curiangu." In *Nós, os bianos*. Mazza Edições, 1996.

Pereira, Edimilson de Almeida, and Núbia Pereira de Magalhães Gomes. *Ardis da imagem: Exclusão étnica e violência nos discursos da cultura brasileira*. 2nd ed. Mazza Edições, 2018.

Pimentel, Evandro. "O Corpo como instrumento da arte: Conheça a performer Val Souza." Red Bull, October 6, 2019. https://www.redbull.com/br-pt/performer-val -souza.

Pinto, Valdina O. "Entrevista" [Interview]. In "A cosmologia africana dos Bantu-Kongo por Bunseki Fu-Kiau: Tradução negra, reflexões e diálogos a partir do Brasil." PhD diss., by Tiganá Santana Neves Santos, Universidade de São Paulo, 2019.

Pomian, Krzysztof. "Tempo/temporalidade." In *Tempo/temporalidade*, translated by Maria Bragança. Enciclopédia Einaudi 29. Imprensa Nacional; Casa da Moeda, 1993.

Portal Geledés. "'Alguma coisa a ver com uma missão,' da Cia. Os Crespos convida espectador a revisitar lutas negras no Brasil." October 26, 2016. https://www.geledes.org.br /alguma-coisa-ver-com-uma-missao-da-cia-os-crespos-convida-espectador-revisitar -lutas-negras-no-brasil/.

Queiroz, Sônia. *Pé preto no barro branco: A língua dos negros na Tabatinga*, 2nd ed. Editora UFMG, 2019.

Reis, José Carlos. *Tempo, história e evasão*. Papirus, 1994.

Ribeiro, Stephanie. "Quem somos: Mulheres negras no plural, nossa existência é pedagógica." In *Explosão feminista: Arte, cultura, política e universidade*, edited by Heloisa Buarque de Hollanda. Companhia das Letras, 2018.

Ricoeur, Paul. *A memória, a história, o esquecimento*. Translated by Alain François et al. Editora da UNICAMP, 2007.

Ricoeur, Paul. "Introdução" [Introduction]. In *As culturas e o tempo: Estudos reunidos pela Unesco*, edited by Paul Ricoeur, translated by Gentil Titton. Editora da USP, 1975.

Ricoeur, Paul. *Tempo e narrativa*. 3 vols. Translated by Roberto Leal Ferreira. Papirus, 1997.

Risério, Antônio. *Oriki Orixá*. Perspectiva, 1996.

Risério, Antônio. *Textos e tribos*. Imago, 1993.

Roach, Joseph. *Cities of the Dead: Circum-Atlantic Performance*. Columbia University Press, 1996.

Roach, Joseph. "Culture and Performance in the Circum-Atlantic World." In *Performativity and Performance*, edited by Andrew Parker and Eve Sedgwick. Routledge, 1995.

Roberts, Mary N., and Allen F. Roberts. "Body Memory Part 1: Defining the Person." In *Memory: Luba Art and the Making of History*, edited by Mary Nooter Roberts and Allen F. Roberts. Museum for African Art; Prestel, 1996.

Rodrigues, Graziela Estela Fonseca. *Bailarino-pesquisador-intérprete: Processo de formação*. 2nd ed. Funarte, 2005.

Roubine, Jean-Jacques. *Introdução às grandes teorias do teatro*. Translated by André Telles. Jorge Zahar Editor, 2003.

Rovelli, Carlo. *A ordem do tempo*. Translated by Silvana Cobucci. Objetiva, 2018.

Rui, Manuel. *Eu e o outro—o invasor (ou em três poucas linhas uma maneira de pensar o texto)*. Centro Cultural, 1985.

Samain, Etienne. "As imagens não são bolas de sinuca. Como pensam as imagens." In *Como pensam as imagens*, edited by Etienne Samain. Editora da UNICAMP, 2012.

Santana, Tiganá. "Tradução, interações, e cosmologias africanas." *Cadernos de Tradução* 39 (September–December 2019): 65–77.

Santos, Deoscóredes Maximiliano dos, and Juana E. Santos. *African Sacred Arts and Rituals in Brazil*. Institute of African Studies, 1967.

Santos, Inaicyra Falcão dos. *Corpo e ancestralidade: Uma proposta pluricultural de dança-arte-educação*. EDUFBA, 2002.

Santos, Juana Elbein dos. *Os Nagô e a morte: Pàde, Àsèsè e o culto Ègum na Bahia*. 5th ed. Vozes, 1988.

Santos, Tiganá Santana Neves. "A cosmologia africana dos Bantu-Kongo por Bunseki Fu-Kiau: Tradução negra, reflexões e diálogos a partir do Brasil." PhD diss., Universidade de São Paulo, 2019.

Saturnino, Andrea Caruso. "Ligeiro deslocamento do real: Experiência, dispositivo e utopia na cena contemporânea." PhD diss., Universidade de São Paulo, 2017.

Schechner, Richard. *Between Theater and Anthropology*. University of Pennsylvania Press, 1985.

Schechner, Richard. "O que é performance." *O percevejo—Revista de Teatro, Crítica e Estética* 11, no. 12 (2003): 25–50.

Schechner, Richard. *Performance Theory*. Revised and enlarged ed. Routledge, 1994.

Schechner, Richard, and Willa Appel, eds. *By Means of Performance, Intercultural Studies and Ritual*. Cambridge University Press, 1993.

Sérgio, Lucélia. "A cena mineira: Memória, identidade e protagonismo em BH." *Legítima Defesa, uma Revista de Teatro Negro* 2, no. 2 (2016): 34–47.

Silva, Eusébio Lôbo da (Mestre Pavão). *O corpo na capoeira*. Editora UNICAMP, 2008.

Silva, Salloma Salomão Jovino da. "Apresentação" [Foreword]. In *Negras insurgências: teatros e dramaturgias negras em São Paulo; perspectivas históricas, teóricas e práticas*, edited by Salloma Salomão Jovino da Silva. Capulanas Cia. de Arte Negra, 2018.

Sklar, Deidre. *Dancing with the Virgin: Body and Faith in the Fiesta of Tortugas, New Mexico*. University of California Press, 2001.

Sodré, Muniz A. C. *A verdade seduzida*. Ed. Francisco Alves, 1988.

Sodré, Muniz A. C. *Pensar nagô*. Vozes, 2017.

Sodré, Muniz A. C. *Samba, o dono do corpo*. 2nd ed. Mauad, 1998.

Souza, Juliana Rosa de. "Reflexões sobre o teatro negro: Uma análise a partir de textos teatrais contemporâneos de autoria negra." PhD diss., Universidade do Estado de Santa Catarina, 2019.

Soyinka, Wole. *Myth, Literature and the African World*. Cambridge University Press, [1976] 1995.

Soyinka, Wole. "Theatre in African Traditional Cultures: Survival Patterns." In *The Twentieth-Century Performance Reader*, edited by Michael Huxley and Noel Witts. Routledge, 1996.

Tavares, Júlio, ed. *Gramáticas das corporeidades afrodiaspóricas, perspectivas etnográficas*. Appris Editora, 2020.

Taylor, Diana. *The Archive and the Repertoire: Performing Cultural Memory in the Americas*. Duke University Press, 2003.

Taylor, Diana. "Hacia una definición de performance." *O Percevejo—Revista de Teatro, Crítica e Estética* 11, no. 12 (2003): 17–24.

Thompson, Robert Farris. *African Art in Motion: Icon and Act*. University of California Press, 1979.

Thompson, Robert Farris. *Flash of the Spirit: African and African-American Art and Philosophy*. Vintage Books, 1984.

Tonezzi, José, and Guilherme Schulte. "Cena, tecnologia e inovação: Desafios para a formação da pesquisa em artes e espetáculo." *Moringa, Artes do Espetáculo, Dossiê Cena e Tecnologia* 2, no. 1 (2011): 51–60. https://periodicos.ufpb.br/ojs2/index.php/moringa/article/view/9983/5463.

Turner, Victor. *From Ritual to Theatre: The Human Seriousness of Play*. PAJ, 1982.

Vargas, D. "Vows to Saints." In *Encyclopedia of Latin American Religions*, edited by Henri Gooren. Springer, 2016. https://doi.org/10.1007/978-3-319-08956-0_199-1.

Vernant, Jean-Pierre. *A morte nos olhos, figurações do outro na Grécia antiga, Artemis e Gorgó*. Translated by Clóvis Marques. Jorge Zahar Editor, 1988.

Vieira, José Luandino. "Lá em Tetembuatuba." In *No antigamente da vida: Estórias*, 4th ed. Edições 70, 1987.

Villas Bôas, Rafael. "*Cidade Vodu*: A disposição de correr riscos entre fronteiras." *Cadernos de Ensaios* 8, no. 2 (2016): 21–28.

Vogt, Carlos, and Peter Fry. *Cafundó, a África no Brasil: Linguagem e sociedade.* Editora da UNICAMP, 2013.

Zumthor, Paul. *A letra e a voz: A "literatura" medieval.* Translated by Amálio Pinheiro and Jerusa Pires Ferreira. Companhia das Letras, 1993.

Zumthor, Paul. *Introdução à poesia oral.* Translated by Jerusa Pires Ferreira, Maria Lúcia Diniz Pochat, and Maria Inês de Almeida. Hucitec, 1997.

Zumthor, Paul. *Performance, recepção, leitura.* Translated by Jerusa Pires Ferreira and Suely Fenerich. Editora da PUC-SP, 2000.

Index

Note: *Page numbers followed by f refer to figures.*

being, 1, 28–29, 31, 47–48, 88, 105, 113; Africa and, 18; ancestral aesthetics of, 34; being-in-the-world, 87; body and, 20; canvas-body and, 39; in-being, 108; Mnemosyne and, 57; patterns in, 25; pleasure of, 36; style of, 32; ways of, 15

Bergson, Henri, 5

Black cultures, 18, 32, 57, 70, 74, 101; in the Americas, 62, 73; in Brazil, 73; crossroads and, 22; distorted images of, 85; ethics of, 34, 112; music and dance and, 44, 110; musicality in, 50; ritual ceremonies and, 19

Blackness, 52, 71, 79, 82, 85–86, 89, 102–3

Black people, 21, 67, 102; achievements of, 82; Blackness and, 79; Brazilian stage and, 83; chants and, 13, 52; distorted images of, 85; enslaved, 19, 69; funerals in New Orleans and, 30; images of, 86; racism against, 89; violence against, 98

Bosi, Alfredo, 5, 8–9, 39, 94

Brazil, 6, 90; African culture in, 62; *africanias* in, 121n48; African languages in, 122n63; African musical heritage in, 51; art in, 86; Bantu languages in, 54, 122–23n63; Black conviviality territories in, 125n56; Black cultures in, 73; Black people in, 79; Black women in, 92; burial rituals in, 30; enslaved Black people in, 19; family in, 27; Haiti and, 98; intellectuals in, 15; Kalunga in, 26; Nago philosophical wisdom in, 22; social issues in, 83. *See also* Minas Gerais

breath, 1, 48–50, 71; ancestors', 48, 67; divine, 1, 70, 111; sacred, 107, 111, 113

Caixa Preta, 95, 97, 100

calendars, 3–4, 8

call and response, 35, 46, 51–52, 105, 112

Candombes, 47, 67

Candomblé, 27, 47, 58, 88, 120n29; Angola Nation, 54; liturgy, 101. See also *terreiros*

canvas-body, 39–40, 57–59, 74, 84–85, 89, 95, 102–3

capoeira, 29, 43, 47, 121n17

caranda, 31, 120n44

Carlos, Dione, 90

ceremonies, 12–13, 15, 19, 70; celebration, 72; funeral, 31

chants, 12, 20, 50–54, 62, 117n1, 121n8, 124n13; Africa and, 41; ancestors and, 48; *congadeiros* and, 13, 76; *Moçambiqueiros* and, 67; Passô and, 96; Reinados, 49, 70, 72

choreography, 3, 58, 63, 67, 111, 120n18; of alterity, 102; of diversity, 102; of gestures, 95; of returns, 41; of voice, 12

chronology, 1, 4, 16; linear, 73

Chronos, 4–5

chronosophy, 4, 16

clothing, 28, 34, 55–56, 123n3; all-white, 67; military, 98

Cobra, Hilton, 81

community, 2, 21, 25, 35, 47; *majestades* and, 67–68; members, 51, 54; ritual repetition and, 50; surrogation and, 63

completeness, 57, 108–9. *See also* incompleteness

congadeiros, 13, 70, 73–74

Congados, 13, 41, 52, 73, 88, 118n26, 119n18, 123n5; *embaixadas* and, 52, 122n56

Congos, 23, 64, 66

Connerton, Paul, 15, 56

continuity, 21, 57; of existence, 73; life, 25, 35, 107, 109; symbolic, 50

contraction, 3, 29, 106, 110; temporal, 41

Couto, Mia, 17, 107

culture, 2, 8, 25, 32–33, 36, 54, 112; African, 11, 35; autochthonous, 52; Bantu, 6; body and, 45; Brazilian, 29, 74, 82; crossroads, 22; semiotic production of, 43; tradition and, 20. *See also* Black cultures

crossroads, 18, 21–24, 49, 51, 63, 109, 113. See also *nzilas*

Cunha, Henrique, Júnior, 25, 34–35, 58

curved temporalities, 3, 111

dance, 13–14, 28, 44, 81, 88, 96, 110–11; Africa and, 71; capoeira and, 43; *ciranda*, 120n44; *corridinhos*, 122n54; *kizomba*, 123n73; Kongo, 41; language and, 71; Moçambique, 65, 67; Orishas and, 45; Reinados and, 64; ritual performance and, 46

dances, 12, 20, 29, 63, 66–67; African-inspired, 109; Black ritual, 46; circle, 120n19; clothing and, 55; Congo, 64; *majestades* and, 68;

memory of knowledge and, 72; Moçambique, 42; Orisha, 45; performative possibilities of, 100; Reinado ceremony and, 70, 72; urban, 88

death, 26, 30–32, 63, 72–73, 107, 111

De Chocolat, 81

Descartes, René, 6

Didi-Huberman, Georges, 21, 35, 57, 102

dilatation, 3, 29

discontinuity, 3, 89

displacement, 63, 67–68, 82, 87, 99; the Americas and, 18; Black cultures and, 57, 70; the body and, 92; rites and, 20, 72

drama, 44, 97

drums, 12–13, 26, 41–42, 47–48, 51, 64–67, 69; African, 18–19; *candombes*, 73; *tambores de mineiros*, 88

duration, 5, 9, 14, 37, 102

embaixadas, 52, 64, 66, 122n56

embodied practices, 2, 43, 71, 85, 109; African-referenced, 121n13; Black, 40, 42, 84; canvas-body and, 39; writing and, 11

embodiment, 10, 13, 15

ephemerality, 14, 31, 57

Èsù, 22–23

ethos, 28, 67–68

fabulations, 6–7, 66, 69, 79, 87–88, 100

family, 27

Fu-Kiau, Bunseki, 5, 17, 71, 120n20

Galard, Jean, 44, 97

Gates, Henry Louis, Jr., 23

gender, 87; relations, 82

gestas, 37, 39, 47, 51, 85, 102

gesture, 19, 42–46, 49–50, 68, 71–74, 90, 96–97; of becoming, 107; Blackness as, 103; knowledge and, 3, 15; memory as, 112–13; of realization, 34

ginga, 42, 121n17

giras, 24, 40–42

gnosis, 16, 105; African, 70; Black, 18

graffiti, 16, 40

graphyas, 3, 37, 112, 117n3; alphabetic writing as, 10; of embodied knowledges, 15, 40; ritual

performance as, 46; sonorities as, 71; of the voice, 47; of wisdoms, 15–16

griot, 44, 51–53, 62

guardas, 63, 65–67, 69, 123n3

Hegel, G. W. F., 5, 10

heritage, 17, 53, 101; African, 27; Black-African, 83; Black-African musical, 51; cultural, 50

Hesiod, 4

history, 10–11, 34, 49, 51, 53, 62, 74, 84, 111; of Africa, 101; art, 41, 71; art and, 86; of Bantu peoples, 6, 25; Black, 52, 57, 66, 99; of Brazilian theater, 102; of forgetting, 12; language and, 7; *oralitura* and, 15; of philosophy, 5; of Reinados, 70

Hobbes, Thomas, 6

improvisation, 21, 52, 57, 113

incompleteness, 57, 112

Indigenous peoples, 11–12, 17, 46, 100

instruments (musical), 18, 51–52, 57; African, 19; from Mali, 34; percussion, 47–48, 111. See also *atabaques*; drums

Jones, LeRoi, 34, 47, 51, 54

Jongo, 29, 47, 88

Kalunga, 24, 26, 34, 59, 108–9

Kant, Immanuel, 5–6

Kikongo, 41, 73

kinesis, 20, 26–27, 40, 48, 105, 108–9

kizomba, 58, 123n73

knowledge, 3–6, 9–16, 18–26, 46, 62, 70–73, 76, 84–86, 112–13; African, 63, 72, 110; Africanity and, 53; *afrografias* and, 121n13; alternate, 57, 68, 89; ancestors and, 106–8, 118n26; Black aesthetic-cultural, 100–101; Black culture and, 32; Black people and, 80; body and, 74, 110; cartographies, 112; cosmic, 35; cultural, 2; effective, 29; *graphyas* of, 40, 112; hegemonic, 67; intimate, 92; memory of, 15, 20, 72, 109; *oralituras* and, 39; production of, 2; spoken word and, 49; of time, 52

percussion, 47–48, 51, 54, 111. *See also* instruments (musical)

performance, 2, 14, 22, 32, 43–44, 49, 68, 74; body and, 3, 12, 72, 110, 112–13; cultural, 118n26; gesture and, 97; of memory, 12; mythopoetic, 64; oral, 9; *oralitura* and, 16, 48; of oral textuality, 50; parameters of, 101; practices, 13, 84, 112, 121n48; text and, 70, 96. *See also* call and response; ritual performance

Performance Studies, 13–14

permanence, 20, 31–33, 36, 57, 106–7, 109, 112

personhood, 88; Black, 102

philosophy, 3–6, 12, 25–26, 56; African, 6, 9, 26, 35, 70; Bantu, 28; collective, 34; Western, 6

poetics, 14, 95; ancestral, 91; of Black aesthetics, 83; Black embodied practices and, 84; of Black theater, 94; of the body, 33, 71; of the canvas-body, 39–40, 85; concretist, 96; contemporary, 80; firefly, 100, 102; of gestures, 43, 100, 110; Glissant's, 99; griot, 52; of ritual performances, 33; techno-digital, 101; visibility, 39

poetry, 8, 28, 44, 51, 89; of the act, 44, 97; Oriki-poems, 53

poiesis, 96; autopoiesis, 43; of movement, 44, 97, 110

polychromy, 56, 95, 110

Portuguese language, 117n1, 117nn3–4, 118n26, 121n1, 121n8, 122n34, 124n13, 125n45; Brazilian, 54, 120n20, 122n63, 123n6

presence, 14, 20, 32, 57–58, 87, 102, 107; ancestors and, 26, 29, 106, 109, 111; belonging and, 113; divine, 24, 59. *See also* absence

pronunciations, 46–51, 54, 71, 92, 111; expressive, 95; sacred, 67

proverbs, 25, 35, 51, 53; African, 53, 58

quilombolas, 57, 70, 123n72

quilombos, 86, 91, 125n20

racism, 82, 84, 89, 92, 96, 100

rebolejo, 42, 121n16

reception, 82; of images, 39; orality and, 14; of performance, 16

Reinados, 63, 66, 70, 119n18; Black, 63, 67, 69;

burial rituals and, 30–31; celebrations of, 27, 64; chants of, 49, 52–53; choreographies of, 73; crossroads and, 23; nature and, 59; performances of, 70, 72; poles, 58; three and, 47. *See also* Congados

Reis, José Carlos, 5

relaxation, 3, 29, 106

religion, 101, 113; African, 21, 58, 100, 119n3; African American, 119n3; African-based, 25, 28; African Brazilian, 73, 110; Bantu-based, 30; Brazilian, 71; Catholic, 119n18; Latin American, 123n7

religious systems, 22, 29, 63, 109, 119n18

resurrection, 31, 107

reversibility, 3, 5, 8–9, 23, 68, 106

Rezende, Priscila, 91, 94*f*

rhythm(s), 8–9, 42–43, 46–47, 50, 64, 67, 72, 110–12; African, 48; body language and, 19; drums and, 47–48; language and, 71; sonorities and, 95; visualizations of, 44; of vocality, 3

Ricoeur, Paul, 6–9

ritornellos, 8–9, 102, 105, 111, 117n1

ritual, 2, 16, 22, 24, 26, 28–31, 49–50, 59; Black practices of, 95; ceremonies, 19; dances, 46; funeral, 31; as model, 72; Reinados and, 66, 70; repertoire, 100; repetition, 50; sacredness and, 68; social, 34; speculations, 4; words, 50

ritual performance, 14, 19–20, 33, 41, 45–46, 48, 73; African-style, 63; Black, 43; of Reinados, 70

Roach, Joseph, 12, 14, 19, 30, 63, 70

Rocha, Sanara, 18*f*, 98

Rodrigues, Graziela, 41, 45

sacred, the, 1, 13, 23, 29, 70, 113; Kalunga as place of, 26; *majestades* and, 68; nature and, 58. *See also* breath

sacredness, 24–25, 27, 32, 51, 59, 68

Salomão, Salloma, 82–83

Samain, Etienne, 39, 85

samba, 29, 42, 51

Santana, Tiganá, 34, 120n20

Santos, Juana Elbein dos, 22, 47, 49

São Paulo, 97–98, 125n33, 125n56

Sasa, 30

Schechner, Richard, 13

Sergio, Lucelia, 55f, 83, 88
silence, 2, 83, 85, 91, 96
simultaneity, 3, 5, 8, 113
skin, 3, 12, 56–57, 69, 91, 95, 103; inscriptions, 110
slavery, 27, 51, 62, 64–65, 68, 84–85, 89
slave system, 57, 70
Sodre, Muniz A. C., 23, 28, 42, 44, 47, 50, 71, 110
sophyas, 3, 16, 25–27, 34, 108, 112, 117n3
Souza, Val, 90, 92
Soyinka, Wole, 63, 120n39
spirals, 3, 9, 16, 42, 47, 102; of ancestrality, 52; of ancestral time, 108; of concentration and distribution, 31; of memory, 4; of time, 26, 46, 73, 105, 113
subjectivities, 16, 82, 85, 88, 90; encapsulated, 83, 88
succession, 4–6, 9
synchronicity, 29, 91
syncopation, 42–43, 51

Taylor, Diana, 11, 14
Teatro Experimental do Negro (Black Experimental Theater), 81, 100
Teatro Popular Solano Trindade, 81, 100
temporality, 1, 3–5, 9, 29, 73; action as, 46; ancestral, 107; Kalunga, 108; mythical, 47–48; space and, 45; spiral, 73, 91; of the subject, 23; transient, 26
terreiros, 27, 59, 91, 120n29; Black, 58, 62
theater, 13–14, 81, 86, 90–91, 100–102; Black, 79, 83, 86, 94, 102; Brazilian, 79, 89, 102
Theater of the Real, 84
Thompson, Robert Farris, 27, 34, 41, 44, 56, 71
time, 1–11, 14–16, 26, 29–30, 41–48, 51–54, 63–64, 71–74, 105–6, 108–13; canvas-body and, 102; linear, 5; Macro-Time, 30; Micro-Time, 30; *ntangu*, 41, 105; ontology of, 23; as ritornello, 8; space and, 45, 74, 97; tradition and, 34; words and, 7; as writing, 6
tradition, 20–21, 33–35, 42, 57; Black aes-

thetic, 102; circuit of, 48; of elapsed time, 29; Judeo-Christian, 9; Nago-Yoruba, 25; theatrical, 89; transmission of, 73
Turner, Victor, 20, 64, 72

Umbandas, 58, 88

violence, 84–85, 98; institutionalized, 100
vocality, 3, 12, 51, 54, 58, 92, 96
voice, 1, 3, 19, 46–52, 67–68, 71, 76, 82, 91–92, 95–96, 111; African, 69; of ancestrality, 74; Black ritual practices and, 95; choreography of, 12; *graphyas* and, 3, 15, 47; inventory, 84; memory and, 112; percussion and, 54, 111; performance of, 62; personalized, 85, 97; poetic, 109; poetics of, 14; ritual performances and, 33; solfeggios, 100; wisdom and, 10

West, the, 4, 8–9, 19, 35
wisdom, 2–3, 10–16, 19–22, 24, 109–13, 117n3; African, 20, 22, 72, 110; Bantu, 23; Black, 103; body and, 40, 50, 71, 95, 110; cartographies, 54; collective, 47; Indigenous, 17; medicinal, 29; orality and, 52; *oralitura* and, 112; words and, 49
women, 89, 91–92; African American, 93; Black, 82, 89, 91–92, 98–99; young, 35
writing, 10–11, 19, 50, 112, 117n3; alphabetic, 10–11; dancing and, 41; hieroglyphic, 43, 97; knowledge and, 3; memory and, 8; orality and, 9, 13, 15–16; scripture as, 117n2; syntax of, 56; time and, 6, 105

Yoruba, 25, 28; cosmologies, 29; language, 99; people, 34, 57; philosophical-religious system, 22; sign interpretation system, 23; traditions, 56

Zamani, 30
Zumthor, Paul, 14, 43–44, 48–49, 85, 96–97

www.ingramcontent.com/pod-product-compliance
Lightning Source LLC
Chambersburg PA
CBHW071104280326
41928CB00051B/2822